Essays on Nature and Landscape

SUSAN FENIMORE COOPER

Essays on
Nature and Landscape

Edited by ROCHELLE JOHNSON
and DANIEL PATTERSON

Foreword by John Elder

THE UNIVERSITY OF GEORGIA PRESS
Athens and London

Printed in the United States of America

06 05 04 03 02 C 5 4 3 2 1

06 05 04 03 02 P 5 4 3 2 1

Library of Congress Cataloging-in-Publication Data

Cooper, Susan Fenimore, 1813–1894.

Essays on nature and landscape / Susan Fenimore Cooper ;

edited by Rochelle Johnson and Daniel Patterson.

p. cm.

Includes bibliographical references (p.   ).

ISBN 0-8203-2421-3 (hardcover : alk. paper)—ISBN 0-8203-2422-1 (pbk. : alk. paper)

1. Natural history. 2. Country life. I. Johnson, Rochelle. II. Patterson, J. Daniel. III. Title.

QH81.C768 2002

508—dc21   2001008269

British Library Cataloging-in-Publication Data available

Contents

Foreword

A CENTRAL ACHIEVEMENT of the recent scholarship in environmental literature has been rediscovering neglected authors who still have much to contribute to the conversation of nature and culture. The renewed attention to Susan Fenimore Cooper's writing has been one of the most dramatic cases in point. Not only has she become widely recognized as a pioneer practitioner of American nature writing, but her approach also feels remarkably pertinent to our concerns today. As Cooper reflects upon both the natural history and the human doings of her rural community, she adopts what might now be called a bioregional perspective. She also anticipates the current struggle to connect conversation more directly with the creation of a just and sustainable society.

Cooper's most celebrated work, *Rural Hours*, was reissued numerous times following its publication in 1850. But until Rochelle Johnson and Daniel Patterson's 1998 edition, the last unabridged printing had been in 1876. Making the original text available was essential to the reevaluation of Cooper's writing. Along with the efforts of a growing group of Cooper scholars, it helped establish *Rural Hours* as a book that links Gilbert White and the English naturalist tradition with the work of Thoreau—as well as being an important influence on *Walden* in its own right.

Rediscovering an author (like charting the literature of nature as a whole) is a concentric, not a linear, process; it advances through widening circles of association and awareness. The present collection of Cooper's nature essays both enriches the historical context within which we can encounter *Rural Hours* and enhances our sense of her surprising currency. Two of the most striking themes that emerge here, in both regards, are those of inheritance and American identity. It is perhaps not surprising that inheritance should be on the mind of an author whose father and literary advisor was the most celebrated American writer of the day. The fact that the hamlet she chronicled in *Rural Hours* was named Cooperstown further strengthened her awareness of being the inheritor of an important legacy, and her adoption of her father's middle name in adulthood reflected a determination to carry it on. Cooper's appreciation for both her town and her national culture were also heightened by the fact that she was educated in Europe from the age of thirteen. She only returned to her ancestral village and began her career as a writer when she was twenty. In effect, she wrote both as a native and, like her successors in American nature writing John Muir and Mary Austin, as one who discovered and fell in love with her chosen place on Earth as an adult. She spent the rest of her life making it fully her own.

One of many engaging pieces in the present collection is Cooper's introduction to the 1853 American edition of Knapp's *Journal of a Naturalist*. In discussing this work as an offspring of White's *Natural History of Selborne*, and in implicitly connecting herself to the same line, she affirms a transatlantic tradition that runs through her own book, and that continues on through *Walden* into the flourishing nature writing of our day. But she also emphasizes the need for such literature to become fully naturalized in its new continent. In particular, Cooper observes in her introduction that, because Americans' ideas of nature in her time have so often been formed by reading English literature, they frequently confuse English species with the birds and animals of North America. As a way of escaping from this "dream-like phantasmagoria," she suggests that "We may all, if we choose, open our eyes to the beautiful and wonderful realities of the world we live in. Why should we any longer walk blindfold through the fields?" Such a call for vividly seeing what is actually around us both connects Cooper with the emphasis on vision by our contemporary Annie Dillard and anticipates the way in which Barry Lopez sees an informed sensitivity to our own home landscapes as the beginning of a truly "American geography."

Cooper's dedication to a localized natural history also contributes to her writing's notably civic emphasis. It is clear to her, as a meticulous observer, that certain human practices have the effect of either enhancing or undermining the vitality of the community. In paying attention to the bird species that return to her Cooperstown home each year, she notes with alarm the declining numbers of such common species as "robins, wrens, cat-birds, and humming-birds" and becomes fearful for the larger health of her region. "Birds Then and Now" (included here in a cluster of essays called "Otsego Leaves") conveys an elegiac, politically charged voice strikingly similar to much contemporary nature writing. As Cooper reports upon the remarkable diminishment in the numbers of both summer and winter birds over a period of twenty years and speculates about the possible causes of such a falling off, her analysis is remarkably prescient. She calls attention to the devastating effects of unrestricted, year-round hunting. She draws a connection between declining bird populations in upstate New York and human depredations in those species' southern migratory range. And she becomes an early, eloquent voice decrying the use of bird wings in decorating women's hats. This last criticism contributed significantly to a crusade that, in the following decades, led both to the protection of America's native birds and to the formation of important advocacy groups.

A spirit of conservation that grows out of lifelong dedication to one's own place on Earth, but always relates that community to broader circles of culture and to the wider migrations of local wildlife, offers a valuable model for us today. In our literature and our environmental activism alike, we are now called upon to find such an inclusive vision, one that incorporates wilderness preservation, sustainability, and social inclusiveness. Because of her own attentive and comprehensive approach as a writer, Susan Fenimore Cooper may become as important to our future thinking about literature and nature as she has been influential upon it in the past.

JOHN ELDER

Acknowledgments

HUGH C. MACDOUGALL sent us a message one day in 1998 saying he had come across a series of essays entitled "Otsego Leaves" that Susan Cooper had published in 1878. Recognizing the high quality of these forgotten essays, we saw that Hugh had made a significant discovery for the history of American nature writing. We thank Hugh for—once again—sharing his findings with us.

Barbara Ras of the University of Georgia Press encouraged us in this project from our first suggestion of it to her, and we are grateful to her for so pleasantly creating a home for Susan Cooper studies at the University of Georgia Press. We feel fortunate to work with Barbara and her colleagues.

The University of Virginia's Alderman Library has granted us permission to publish from the Susan Cooper letters in their collection, for which we are grateful.

Introduction

WHEN Susan Fenimore Cooper (b. April 17, 1813; d. December 31, 1894) published *Rural Hours* in 1850, she became one of the most accomplished nature writers in the United States.[1] Her literary representation of a year in the life of her Otsego Lake region (including its flora, fauna, climate, economy, geology, and human inhabitation) received unanimous praise from the reviewers for clarity, grace, and purity. In 1850, however, she was yet at the beginning of a prodigious literary career that spanned fifty years, beginning with her only novel, *Elinor Wyllys*, in 1845 and concluding with a children's short story published in *St. Nicholas* magazine in January of 1895, shortly after her death on the last day of 1894. Although nature writing was only one of the many genres in which she worked, it is the genre to which she returned most often.[2] At the end of her career, her contributions to American nature writing stood as the dominant voice amid all her literary production.

During this second half of the nineteenth century, tremendous changes occurred in practically every aspect of American society, and throughout all of these changes, Susan Cooper maintained in her essays on landscape and nature a literary vigil for her two great themes: the idealization of American rural life and advocacy for an environmentally sustainable human society.

Collectively, the essays reissued here compose a full portrait of her thought on nature and how humans should live and think in relation to nature. Her best known work of nature writing, *Rural Hours*, is clearly designed to perform the cultural work of this genre, but nowhere in the book does the author explicitly discuss her theory or conception of nature writing as a genre. The degree of self-consciousness needed for such a discussion would have been distracting, even indecorous, in a work she later indirectly likened to those of Gilbert White and

John Leonard Knapp, works "written neither for fame nor for profit, but which have opened spontaneously, one might almost say unconsciously, from the author's mind."[3] When one reads the rest of her environmental writings, however, the fullness of her environmental philosophy becomes clear, as does her fifty-year commitment to issues concerning environmental history, sustainable landscape and community design, and the preservation of what we now refer to as biodiversity. Each essay in this collection helps clarify one or more aspects of Susan Cooper's environmental thought.

During a seven-year period that spans from 1848, when Cooper began the journal entries that became *Rural Hours*, until 1855, with the publication of *The Rhyme and Reason of Country Life*, Cooper developed, logically and explicitly, her theory of nature writing as well as her philosophy of nature.

Following *Rural Hours*, Cooper published a full statement of her theory of landscape aesthetics, "A Dissolving View."[4] Here she articulates succinctly and directly an environmental principle that informs the earlier book: "The hand of man generally improves a landscape. The earth has been given to him, and his presence in Eden is natural; he gives life and spirit to the garden." Cooper follows this idea, which echoes the aesthetic theory of Thomas Cole and other landscape painters of the Hudson River School, with a warning: "It is only when he endeavors to rise above his true part of laborer and husbandman, when he assumes the character of creator, and piles you up hills, pumps you up a river, scatters stones, or sprinkles cascades, that he is apt to fail" (6). Thus in her only essay devoted exclusively to landscape aesthetics, Cooper calls for a comfortable balance, a sustainable human presence on the land, a human relation to the physical environment that allows for a picturesque and necessary human presence but which does not deplete the resources beyond the land's capacity to give without diminishing its health. The author ties her landscape aesthetic directly to the ecological health of the land.

Cooper also characterizes the place of village life in a suggestive way, writing: "We are the borderers of civilization in America" (12). By "borderers" she means pioneers, those advancing civilization into the wilderness, but her valuation of village life relative to city life remains laden with ambiguity in the paragraph that grows out of this opening statement, as does the essay's contrasting presentations of American and European landscapes in its conclusion (14–16). This apparent ambiguity in Cooper's thought clarifies as she works through her next two projects.

"A Dissolving View" appeared in a costly gift book entitled *The Home Book of the Picturesque: Or American Scenery, Art, and Literature* (1852). The publisher of this volume, George Putnam, promoted Susan Fenimore Cooper (whose *Rural Hours* he was still benefiting from) by letting her share prominence with her father, William Cullen Bryant, and Washington Irving, three of the country's most famous authors, all of whom also contributed essays on American landscape. So privileged a place for "A Dissolving View" reinforced Cooper's status as a new American nature writer and likely encouraged her to conceive and complete the other works of environmental writing she produced through the early 1850s.

In her brief introduction to the American edition of British naturalist John Leonard Knapp's *Journal of a Naturalist* (1829),[5] Cooper reveals some of her thoughts about the purpose of nature writing. One issue she uses this opportunity to address is the pervasive ignorance among her compatriots of native flora and fauna: "As a people, we are still, in some sense, half aliens to the country Providence has given us; there is much ignorance among us regarding the creatures which held the land as their own long before our forefathers trod the soil, and many of which are still moving about us, living accessories of our existence, at the present hour" (20–21). Because of "English reading," Americans habitually assume that plant and animal species are identical on both sides of the Atlantic simply because they have the same names: "And in this dream-like phantasmagoria, where fancy

and reality are often so widely at variance . . . most of us are content
to pass through life" (22). To help remedy this ignorance, Cooper
explains—through fifty pages of natural history notes—the differences between European and North American animals and plants
bearing the same names. Her introduction makes clear that one purpose of nature writing is "to honor the Creator in the study of his
works. It is pleasant to know familiarly the plants which spring up at
our feet; we like to establish a sort of intimacy with the birds which,
year after year, come singing about our homes." Even environmental
writings from foreign places have value and bring pleasure: "[W]hen
told of the wonders of a foreign vegetation, differing essentially from
our own, when hearing of the habits of strange creatures from other
and distant climates, we listen eagerly as to a tale of novelty" (20).
Here, just as she anatomizes her own pleasant experience as a reader
of accounts of regions and countries other than her own, she also suggests a principle that directs her own contributions to the genre of
nature writing: With the ultimate purpose being "to honor the Creator," descriptions of foreign plants or animals can bring the reader
delight comparable to that experienced more commonly when hearing "a tale of novelty." Cooper works subtly in this introduction to
persuade more readers that the genre offers value and pleasure more
often sought in popular genres such as the historical romance, wherein
her father found success.

　More so than any other single document, the introductory essay
Cooper wrote for her anthology of nature poetry, *The Rhyme and
Reason of Country Life* (1855),[6] teems with insights into her thought
and suggests how she understood her place in her culture and her
work as a writer. Cooper suggests that rural nature writers hold one
of the most important places in her culture. Whereas in past ages, the
most influential writers worked from within cities because only there
were people educated (with the result that the "tastes and habits" of
the culture were "necessarily . . . more or less artificial"), in Cooper's
young nation, the much wider dissemination of education and the

other advantages of civilization free the "rustic population" from the
urban perception that they are "only fit for ridicule and burlesque"
(36). Instead, the American intellectual or artist can work effectively
from rural settings. In America, "[t]he influences which surround the
countryman are essentially ennobling, elevating, civilizing, in fact."
She concludes: "It can scarcely, therefore, be an error of judgment to
believe that while in past generations the country has received all its
wisdom from the town, the moment has come when in American society many of the higher influences of civilization may rather be sought
in the fields, when we may learn there many valuable lessons of life,
and particularly all the happy lessons of simplicity" (43–44). In *Rural
Hours* Cooper suggests that accurate literary representations of the
natural can contribute to the "moral and intellectual progress" of the
culture (*Rural Hours*, 208). In this introductory essay to her anthology
of nature poetry, Cooper explains explicitly why she thinks so.

This essay also constitutes one of the most forceful statements of
Cooper's entire career. Through the first portion of the essay, Cooper
surveys ancient, medieval, and modern world literatures and characterizes the place nature held in each. For most of her discussion of this
broad topic, she follows Alexander von Humboldt's compendious account included in his *Cosmos* (1845–62).[7] Humboldt's worldwide repu-
tation as a naturalist had reached its zenith at this time. (Cooper often
felt the frustration of not having needed books at hand in her rural village, so having access to *Cosmos* must have seemed a fortunate luxury
for her, since it contained so much of the known facts of the world.)[8]
Nevertheless, after basing her discussion of nature in the various
literatures from the ancient Greeks to the Chinese largely on Humboldt's presentation, she strikes out on her own when she moves to a
consideration of the Hebrew poets. Humboldt's "sketch of a physical
description of the universe" is secular; it does not endorse Christian
doctrine. In fact, throughout his great synthesizing work, Humboldt
makes practically no reference to the Christian God. In apparent re-
action against this, Cooper develops a minor treatise on the absolute

necessity of divinely revealed truth for a proper and worthy comprehension of the natural world.

Cooper opens her discussion of the Hebrew poets of the Old Testament by distinguishing them "absolutely" from "all profane writers" by virtue of their divine inspiration: "They only, as priests and prophets of the One Living God, beheld the natural world in the holy light of truth. Small as was the space the children of Israel filled among the nations of the earth, the humblest individual of their tribes knew that the God of Abraham was the Lord God of Hosts, and that all things visible were but the works of his hands" (29). Whereas Humboldt attributes recent improvements in literary representations of nature to the rise of comparative geography and believes that the highest achievements in nature writing result when the "poetic element" emanates "from the intuitive perception of the connection between the sensuous and the intellectual,"[9] Cooper maintains: "It is, indeed, revealed truth only which has opened to the human mind views of the creation at all worthy of its dignity" (32). In Humboldt's view, the writer will succeed who—"secure in the possession of the riches of his native language"—presents an account of the direct, careful observation of natural phenomena within an all-subsuming understanding of a harmonious and boundless cosmos.[10] Religious faith is not necessary. For Cooper, religious faith is essential, though not sufficient alone: "A high degree of general education, in connection with the prevalence of Christian religious truth, must always naturally dispose the mind to a more just appreciation of the works of the Deity, as compared with the works of man. The wider our views of each, the higher will be our admiration of the first" (36). Furthermore, she writes, one of the crucial lessons of Christianity is that humankind is "but the steward and priest of the Almighty Father, responsible for the use of every gift," that "even here on earth, within his own domains, his position is subordinate" (38). It is only when one's knowledge is coupled with Christian faith that one can become capable of comprehending or representing nature properly and worthily. While she relies comfortably on Humboldt's knowledge of world literature, then, Cooper argues at length, if also civilly, against his secular world view.

Following this essay's opening idealization of rural life as "essentially ennobling, elevating, civilizing," Cooper concludes her introduction to the world's nature poetry by making several provocative arguments. Following a theory of John Keble (1792–1866), Cooper suggests that "the poetry of rural life" comes to a culture, not in its youth, but in its full maturity. Currently her country, "the latest born of the nations," is in a greater need of rural values than any nation ever: "Probably there never was a people needing more than ourselves all the refreshments, all the solace, to be derived from country life in its better forms" (39–40). While the ambition, speculation, and distractions of city life are spiritually depleting, she finds a sound basis for hope in two observations. First, the prevalent quality of American verse is "a deeply-felt appreciation of the beauty of the natural world" (41). And, second, because of the general extension of education and goods throughout the country, the city is no longer the source of civilizing influences: "We conceive the spirit which pervades country life to-day, to be more truly civilizing in its nature than that which glitters in our towns" (43). Cooper's America, then, stands at a crucial moment in its development. Suffering from the greatest need for nature that any nation has ever experienced, the country is most fortunate in its new valuation of rural life and stands ready to enjoy the literary fruits of a generation of writers nourished away from the cities amid the physically and spiritually healthful influences of rural life. By the end of this bold essay, Cooper has fully laid out her argument for an elevated, even exalted, position for nature writing and nature writers in her culture.

For the first reissue of *Rural Hours* following the close of the Civil War, Susan Cooper wrote a new preface and added seventeen pages of "Later Hours."[11] The main theme of both is the amount of change her rural village has experienced in the preceding twenty years; the tone is one of restrained lamentation balanced by measured consolation.

In the preface, the most severe change looming is that brought by the approaching railroad: "[M]ust we confess the degradation?" In "Later Hours," Cooper explains her environmental, economic, and aesthetic objections to the railroad:

> Many of us are very desirous that the Lake shore should not be broken up, and our beautiful woods devoured by the fiery breath of the iron horse. Wood, not only for fuel, but for lumber, and other useful purposes, is every day becoming more valuable. If the Railroad destroys our forests it will greatly lower the market value of every farm it has shorn in this way. It will render the hills and valleys colder in winter, and dryer in summer. And if the track passes along the bays, and makes stagnant water, it will bring here, as it has done elsewhere, intermittent fevers, and chills and fever, thus far almost unknown here. (61–62)

Despite a positive turn at the end, the preface is largely a lamentation, expressing regret that "progress" (in the forms of telegraph, gas lights, and railroad) has reached even her isolated valley and will now cause a greater distance between her fellow villagers and nature.

The "Later Hours" are dated from May 25 to July 4, 1868, and while most of the entries are similar to the types of entries that comprise the 1850 *Rural Hours*, several seem trite and pedantic. For two of the entries, she lifts passages whole from the natural history notes she wrote for her 1853 edition of Knapp's work. One of them discusses the shades of meaning in two dialect terms that Knapp comments on; the other is a lengthy quotation from a naturalist's account of the skylark (48, 53–54). The presentation of these in the format of her *Rural Hours* nature observations is certainly inconsistent with the earlier work and seems even a violation of the original purpose and tone of *Rural Hours*.

This apparent betrayal, however, may be very telling. Some of her least compelling prose occurs in a polemic on "true education": "True education must influence alike body, mind, heart, and soul. Its teachings are not partial, but general. Its whole action is healthful. It has no exaggerations. It has no false aims. It is never overstrained. It is thorough in every lesson. It is conscientious in every step. It is wise in all its purposes. It goes to the heart of things" (60). This certainly lacks substance. In the next paragraph, however, where she decries the effects of post–Civil War education, Cooper seems to be suppressing a rhetorical panic. In the summer of 1868, ambitions are immoderate, wealth is pursued above all, there is no chance of a quiet contentment in the village, and no one values humility, simplicity, or good manners (61). With the culture gone, in her view, so wrong, to write a critique that thoroughly exposed and analyzed the problems might have tempted the author toward diatribe. This need to suppress may explain why the preceding paragraph is so vapid.

These "Later Hours" reflect the tremendous changes that have come to Cooperstown over the preceding twenty years, but, more, they suggest that the changes have made the unselfconscious observations that make up *Rural Hours* impossible. Considered from this perspective, *Rural Hours* seems the voice of the land in its time, a voice all the more genuine and authentic than it might appear to be without the instructive contrast of the distracted "Later Hours."

The final entry of "Later Hours" is dated July 4, 1868, and marks the third anniversary of the village's first celebration of nationhood following the end of the Civil War. This is Cooper's longest written statement about the war, and its elegiac tone and restrained rhetoric convey a profound sadness that rises to hope for the nation's future. From her account of the loss of so many young men, it is clear that Cooper and others in the village faced the potential for despair. From the fact that Cooper founded both a hospital and an orphanage during these years, it is clear that her belief in the possibility of cultural improvement was strong.[12]

After the troubled tone of "Later Hours," Cooper develops a set of practical, tangible, manageable procedures for improving the fallen condition and prospects of village life. Whereas her introduction to *The Rhyme and Reason of Country Life* presents much of her philosophy of nature and of writing about nature, her magazine essay "Village

Improvement Societies" shows how one might go about maintaining a village culture and landscape imbued by that philosophy.[13] This
is a substantial polemic for improving and maintaining the "physical, moral, and intellectual good of the people" by forming societies
for "village improvement" across the nation (77). Each village's or
town's society would work to assure that a pure and abundant water source is available and unthreatened; that public thoroughfares are
sound, neat, and picturesque; that noxious weeds are controlled; and
that streets and public places are named after native flora, fauna, and
other natural features. Having lamented recent inroads by the new
technologies in the 1868 additions to *Rural Hours*, she now calls Americans to action and suggests a tangible means of opposition. Village life
in America, she writes, by contrast with its degraded analog in Europe,
is "one of the happiest fruits of modern civilization" (66). Nevertheless, because the rural village is now the most important cultural site
in the country, the future of the nation's moral and aesthetic character
depends on improving our villages: "To improve our villages becomes
a matter of even greater importance than to improve our cities" (69).
This essay is a call to action and shows without doubt that she wanted
her ideas—which are more subtly and indirectly promulgated in her
more "literary" writings—implemented in the landscape and in human society.

    The three "Otsego Leaves" essays included in this volume com-
prise Susan Cooper's most mature and fully realized contributions to
American nature writing.[14] By conveying pertinent and complex ecological interdependencies in narrative prose that is vivid, fresh, and
involving, the author seems to meet effectively the main challenge
faced by all environmental writers: that is, how to catch and keep the
interest of a reader in an essay about animals, plants, and the human
relationship to the physical environment. While there is much that is
remarkable about Cooper's "Otsego Leaves," two points in particular stand out in a consideration of her environmental thought: in the

use she makes of information previously published in *Rural Hours*, Cooper transforms that work into a source of environmental history, which she argues was more important than most of her contemporaries suspected; and, in their treatment of birds and bird populations, these three essays become a work of literary ornithology intended to guide others to the work of preserving bird species.

In the opening paragraphs of "The Bird Primeval," Cooper presents her readers with an argument they probably had not considered before: "The history of a wilderness, if entirely accurate—the long record of a savage race, if strictly true—might indeed be of very high import to the civilized world of to-day" (97). She thus becomes one of the earliest advocates in the United States for what would become a new field of study: environmental history. The opening line of "The Bird Mediæval" shows her interest in sources of information about past environmental conditions: "Here and there, in looking over old records or family legends of colonial years, the mediæval period of American story, we gather glimpses of bird-life, somewhat dim and indistinct, perhaps, yet sufficiently clear to have a degree of interest" (87). She sees this history as important but also difficult—or even impossible—to retrieve. Gendering her environmental history as female, Cooper regrets the loss of so much needed knowledge in "The Bird Primeval": "How much could she tell us that we are longing to know, how many marvels could she unfold that we are craving to inquire into! But never a word shall she utter. Hers is a sublime vision, sweeping over a vast continent, and including a past of thousands of years. But she is mute—utterly mute—mute forever. Silence is her doom" (97).

Twenty-eight years passed between the publications of *Rural Hours* and "Otsego Leaves," and in that time the author of both works came to look on the earlier as a source of the environmental history of her home place. *Rural Hours* was originally conceived as a word portrait of present conditions in Cooperstown and its environs, but a generation later it is most usefully viewed, Cooper finds, as a standard against which to measure the degree and direction of the change that has occurred in the region.

Following Cooper's emphasis in "The Bird Primeval" on the difficulty of recovering reliable information about the history of a wilderness, she confidently asserts: "Nevertheless, it is a glimpse into this vast wilderness that we are about to offer you, good reader. And we shall tell you nothing but what is true" (98). She then begins to describe a three-hundred-year-old elm that stood above Lake Otsego before the first Europeans came to the Americas. For her source of "true" information about the largest and oldest elms, she turns to her description of a venerable elm she included in *Rural Hours*:

> There is an elm of great size now standing entirely alone in a pretty field of the valley, its girth, its age, and whole appearance declaring it a chieftain of the ancient race—the "Sagamore elm," as it is called—and in spite of complete exposure to the winds from all quarters of the heavens, it maintains its place firmly. The trunk measures seventeen feet in circumference, and it is thought to be a hundred feet in height; but this is only from the eye, never having been accurately ascertained. The shaft rises perhaps fifty feet without a branch, before it divides, according to the usual growth of old forest trees. Unfortunately, gray branches are beginning to show among its summer foliage, and it is to be feared that it will not outlast many winters more; but if it die tomorrow, we shall have owed a debt of many thanks to the owner of the field for having left the tree standing so long. (*Rural Hours*, 132).

Cooper's record of the "Sagamore elm" provides the dimensions of her imagined, but historically accurate, primeval elm, whose main trunk stood "without a break in the line for seventy feet" (98) and whose "lofty crown . . . had been torn away by a crashing storm," causing "a great rift . . . in the trunk for some twenty feet from the summit" (99). Approximating the more precise "seventeen feet" circumference of the "Sagamore elm," Cooper visualizes that dimension of the more recently constructed elm: "At the height of a man from the root it would have required three stalwart savage hunters to embrace the trunk in its outward girth" (101). Similarly, where she describes her method of monitoring the local—and declining—populations of certain bird species in "Birds Then and Now," Cooper relies on the record of numbers of nests published in *Rural Hours* (322–25), as well as on her counts in the same village trees through the intervening years. Based on this tangible record, she can conclude that the populations of bird species that build their nests in trees have declined by "more than one-third" in the past twenty years. "This is a sad change," she notes, and she can be aware of it because of her notations of information relevant to the history of the local environment (85).

Susan Fenimore Cooper's work is valuable to us in part because in some of it she records the environmental conditions of her region. More than this, however, we see in her essays what was in her day a rare insight: she wanted to teach her culture the value of knowing what a place was like in its original wild state before civilization brought its impact. Hers was an active, articulate voice, from her rural setting, suggesting that we need reliable sources of environmental history if we want to take efficacious steps toward becoming a culture that is environmentally sustainable. Without accurate knowledge of earlier environmental conditions, "speculation" and "ambition" have their way and the result is a culture shaped and driven by the short-term goals of profit and convenience, not by a desire to be good stewards of the land.

In various ways, "Otsego Leaves" strips Cooper of an earlier mask as a "rustic bird-fancier" (*Rural Hours*, 72) and presents her as an amateur ornithologist. When she explains her method of monitoring the number of bird nests in her village, she is describing the fieldwork of an ornithologist. Similarly, when she analyzes the causes and consequences of declining bird populations, as she does in "Birds Then and Now" (85–86), she is a naturalist working for the preservation of bird species by means of written accounts of her close observations.

Indeed, her preservationist goals set her a generation ahead of other ornithologists. This was the age of "collecting." During the decades following the Civil War, the study of natural history focused much more than ever before on the amassing of extensive collections.[15] The example of Elliott Coues, one of the period's most successful ornithologists, will serve to illuminate by way of contrast the kind of bird study Cooper encourages in "Otsego Leaves." Cooper's essays show the value of staying put, of counting and recounting the nests built in the same familiar trees through decades of observation, and of protecting the lives even of individual birds. Dr. Coues, however, in his *Field Ornithology* (1874), advised collectors to "Get over as much ground, both wooded and open, as you can thoroughly examine in a day's tramp, and go out as many days as you can."[16] While Coues did insist that although a "worthy" collector "destroys some" birds, he does so only to advance our knowledge of "Nature" (21). Nevertheless, when considering how many specimens of a species one should take, Coues writes emphatically, "*All you can get*—with some reasonable limitations; say fifty or a hundred of any but the most abundant and widely diffused species. . . . Birdskins are capital" (27). To Cooper's fear that local species were in decline, Coues would have shown little sympathy; he coached the nation's naturalists, when they considered such a possibility, to assume quickly that the species in question must be thriving elsewhere: "Quite as likely, birds that are scarce just where you happen to be, are so only because you are on the edge of their habitat, and are plentiful in more accessible regions" (29). Coues's "Manual of Instruction"—a phrase from its subtitle—clearly intends to train naturalists to ignore or explain away any obstacle to the business of collecting specimens. Just as clearly, it does not encourage the study of local populations.

Cooper's advocacy of bird preservation in "Otsego Leaves" puts her among a small minority of ornithologists, whether professional or amateur, in the latter nineteenth century. No doubt every village, farm, and family had its bird advocate, the one person who watched the life histories of birds and noted their behaviors more closely than anyone else, a person who perhaps even kept a written log of the numbers of nests built every spring in the same familiar trees—but Susan Cooper seems to be the first to have published an account of this method of estimating and monitoring the health of wren, oriole, robin, and catbird populations in one's village. An awareness of this distinction enhances our appreciation of the originality of her "Otsego Leaves" essays. It is also helpful to be reminded that it was not until the second meeting of the newly formed American Ornithological Union, in October of 1884, that any formal discussion of the preservation of bird species occurred among that professional group, and that discussion was limited to a specific concern about terns on the east coast being taken for "millinery purposes."[17] Thus, one of the contributions to the history of American nature writing made by "Otsego Leaves" is its literary ornithology.

Susan Cooper was eighty years old in 1893 when she published the final essay in this collection, "A Lament for the Birds."[18] Here she testifies to the continued decline of her region's bird populations, as well as to the loss of the original forests. Whereas in "The Bird Primeval" she looks back at twenty years of her bird observations, in this final "Lament" she looks back through forty years, and we learn from her references to counting bird nests in this essay that she counted the nests in her village for at least forty-five years. Apparently nothing had stopped, or even slowed, the declining numbers, and she was not hopeful: "After the bright autumn leaves of those years had all dropped from the trees, it was a pleasant habit to walk about the village streets and note the deserted nests in elm or maple. Frequently there were two, three, and occasionally even four and five nests in the same tree. To-day you may perhaps discover one or two nests in a dozen trees" (114). This lyrical catalogue of a diminished biodiversity notes the loss of white pines, swans, and white pelicans, before developing at some length the history and rapid disappearance of the passenger pigeon (which would pass into extinction twenty-one years later).

Drawing once again upon *Rural Hours* as a source of environmental history, Cooper reworks her account of a fog-bound June morning more than forty years before when a "large flock of wild-pigeons became bewildered in the fog" and alighted all about the town, leaving only after the fog dispersed in the morning sun (112). Her message to readers is that this pleasant visitation from a native species will not be repeated and that a realization of this loss should move them to take effective actions to preserve the remaining shreds of the nation's original biodiversity.

The professionalization of the sciences in the United States occurred gradually through the latter decades of the nineteenth century. Before 1860 or so, there were relatively few professional scientists, and most formal societies with interests in science were as literary as they were scientific. Literary gentlemen typically cultivated an interest in one or more of the ever more distinct branches of the natural sciences. Even as late as 1900, the United States Census included an occupational category for "Literary and Scientific Persons."[19] In the late 1840s, then, when Susan Cooper was recording her nature observations and then in 1850 publishing them as *Rural Hours*, wherein she cites the books of numerous other naturalists, she acquires a public persona similar to that of literary scientific writers such as Gilbert White or William Bartram. However, she disavowed any claim to scientific expertise or authoritativeness. In her preface, Cooper states that her book makes "no claim whatever to scientific knowledge" (*Rural Hours*, 3). This quiet, decorous disclaimer suggests that Cooper is troubled a bit by a possibility that her work might be judged, because of the blurred boundary between the literary and the scientific in her day, as a work of science. That such apprehension on her part is justified is perhaps borne out by the attention she received from several scientists after the publication of *Rural Hours*. Her father wrote on December 25, 1850, that his daughter had "reached the honor of . . . having her autograph desired, and some two or three professors have actually written to her letters full of learning, all about birds and flowers."[20] In 1853, however, when she published an edition of John Leonard Knapp's *Journal of a Naturalist* to which she appended extensive notes explaining differences between European and American plant and animal species bearing the same names, her standing as a scientific naturalist could hardly be denied.

When we consider the description she published in "Otsego Leaves" of her method of counting bird nests in this context, we see that Cooper in 1878 was working actively on that boundary between what Nathan Reingold calls "vernacular" and scientific culture.[21] Just as she argues that the rural is now the place whose influences are most civilizing and most in need, so too she implies that the studied observations from the most intelligent and engaged rural minds can help shape her society in needed directions.

In the year of Cooper's death, 1894, Mabel Osgood Wright published *The Friendship of Nature*, a work of nature writing that advocates amateur, but intelligent, ornithology as a means to raising readers' awareness of the natural—an antidote Wright believed her contemporaries needed amid the destructive complications of industrial America.[22] Wright's variety of ornithology also has the preservation of species as its goal. Together with other activists, many of whom were women, Wright helped make the 1890s the decade in which the movement to preserve bird species became a viable force for change.[23] Susan Cooper's written testimony to the need for such change from 1850 to 1893 can be seen to represent the nation's environmental conscience that would not fully awaken until the end of her life and her century.

D. P.

NOTES

1. Susan Fenimore Cooper, *Rural Hours* (New York: Putnam, 1850). Subsequent references to *Rural Hours*, given parenthetically in the text, are to the following edition: Cooper, *Rural Hours*, ed. Rochelle

Johnson and Daniel Patterson (Athens, Ga.: University of Georgia Press, 1998).

2. For a complete list of Cooper's publications, see *Susan Fenimore Cooper: New Essays on "Rural Hours" and Other Works*, ed. Rochelle Johnson and Daniel Patterson (Athens, Ga.: University of Georgia Press, 2001), 267–70.

3. Cooper, introduction to *Country Rambles in England; or, Journal of a Naturalist with Notes and Additions, by the Author of "Rural Hours," Etc., Etc.*, by John Leonard Knapp, ed. Susan Fenimore Cooper (Buffalo, N.Y.: Phinney & Co., 1853), 11.

4. Cooper, "A Dissolving View," in *The Home Book of the Picturesque: Or American Scenery, Art, and Literature* (New York: Putnam, 1852; Gainesville, Fla.: Scholars' Facsimiles & Reprints, 1967), 79–94. Here and throughout the introduction, page numbers given in parentheses refer to the present edition of the texts, not to their original publication.

5. Cooper, introduction to *Country Rambles in England*, 11–20.

6. Cooper, introduction to *The Rhyme and Reason of Country Life: Or, Selections from Fields Old and New*, ed. Susan Fenimore Cooper (New York: Putnam, 1855), 13–34.

7. Cooper used Alexander von Humboldt, *Cosmos: A Sketch of a Physical Description of the Universe*, trans. Elise C. Otté, 5 vols. (1848–65). Page citations given here are to the reprint edition, 2 vols., (Baltimore: Johns Hopkins University Press, 1997). For Humboldt's analysis of nature in world literatures, see *Cosmos*, 2:21–82.

8. As she once wrote to a family friend in New York City, "it frequently happens now-a-days that my fingers are idle, and my patchwork labours at a stand, for the want of some volume to consult, which if it lay within reach would speedily remove the obstacle in my way, and set me at work again." Letter to Mr. Jay, 2 September 1850, MS. 6245-1, box no. 2, Manuscripts Department, University of Virginia Library.

9. Humboldt, *Cosmos*, 2:77–78, 81.

10. Humboldt, *Cosmos*, 2:81.

11. Cooper, preface and "Later Hours," in *Rural Hours* (New York: Putnam, 1868), iii, 523–39.

12. The Thanksgiving Hospital was dedicated on Thanksgiving Day, 1867, and the Orphan House of the Holy Saviour was incorporated in March of 1870. See Susan Fenimore Cooper, "The Thanksgiving Hospital" and "Orphan House of the Holy Saviour," in *A Centennial Offering. Being a Brief History of Cooperstown, with a Biographical Sketch of James Fenimore Cooper*, ed. S. M. Shaw (Cooperstown, N.Y.: *Freeman's Journal* Office, 1886), 180–82 and 182–84.

13. Cooper, "Village Improvement Societies," *Putnam's Magazine*, 4 (September 1869): 359–66.

14. Cooper, "Otsego Leaves I: Birds Then and Now," *Appletons' Journal*, 4 (June 1878): 528–31; Cooper, "Otsego Leaves II: The Bird Mediæval," *Appletons' Journal*, 5 (August 1878): 164–67; Cooper, "Otsego Leaves III: The Bird Primeval," *Appletons' Journal*, 5 (September 1878): 273–77. A fourth essay concludes the series, but because it does not treat the physical environment, we do not include it in this collection: Cooper, "Otsego Leaves IV: A Road-side Post-office," *Appletons' Journal*, 5 (December 1878): 542–46.

15. Mark V. Barrow Jr. refers to this period of intense collecting as "The Culture of Collecting." See his *A Passion for Birds: American Ornithology after Audubon* (Princeton, N.J.: Princeton University Press, 1998), especially 9–19 and 30–36.

16. Elliott Coues, *Field Ornithology* (Salem, Mass.: Naturalists' Agency, 1874), 24.

17. Barrow, *A Passion for Birds*, 111.

18. Cooper, "A Lament for the Birds," *Harper's New Monthly Magazine*, 87 (August 1893): 472–74.

19. Nathan Reingold, "Definitions and Speculations: The Professionalization of Science in America in the Nineteenth Century," in *The*

Pursuit of Knowledge in the Early American Republic, ed. Alexandra Oleson and Sanborn C. Brown (Baltimore: Johns Hopkins University Press, 1976), 33–69, esp. 38–46.

20. James Franklin Beard, ed., *The Letters and Journals of James Fenimore Cooper*, 6 vols. (Cambridge: Harvard University Press, 1960), 6:246.

21. Reingold, "Definitions and Speculations," 39.

22. Mabel Osgood Wright, *The Friendship of Nature: A New England Chronicle of Birds and Flowers* (1894); ed. Daniel J. Philippon (Baltimore: Johns Hopkins University Press, 1998).

23. Barrow, *A Passion for Birds*, 127–34.

Editorial Principles

OUR GOAL, of course, is to present these texts as their author would wish. Since no manuscripts and no subsequent republications are known to survive, we are limited for textual information to the published versions. Therefore, we present here the texts of the published essays, correcting obvious errors. All emendations are noted at the end of the volume.

Since we know that Susan Cooper thought deliberately about punctuation and spelling, we feel confident that she wanted to spell words consistently. For this reason we make her spelling of words consistent in the few cases where inconsistent spellings occur. We decide which spelling of a particular word to use by looking at how she spelled the word in all of her published and unpublished texts. In every case, there are only two spellings of a word in question; in most cases it is clear that one spelling is an aberration and the other the standard spelling in Cooper's practice. "Shakspeare," for example, occurs as "Shakespeare" only twice in Cooper's published work, but numerous times as "Shakspeare." Therefore, we emend the two occurrences of "Shakespeare" in this volume to read "Shakspeare" and note the editorial change in the list of emendations at the back of the volume. When one of the two spellings is not clearly aberrant, we use the spelling in the 1850 *Rural Hours* since it is certain that she corrected page proofs of that text. All emendations are noted.

To determine whether a compound divided at the end of a line should appear as one word or as a hyphenated compound, we look first for other, undivided occurrences of the word in the same text. If none occurs there, we search Cooper's other publications for evidence of her preference for the compound in question. In the very few cases not resolved by this search, we follow Noah Webster's *An American*

Dictionary of the English Language (New York: Harper and Brothers, 1852).

A few editorial decisions warrant a brief explanation. We have supplied those in the textual notes that follow the list of emendations.

Essays on Nature and Landscape

A Dissolving View

AUTUMN is the season for day-dreams. Wherever, at least, an American landscape shows its wooded heights dyed with the glory of October, its lawns and meadows decked with colored groves, its broad and limpid waters reflecting the same bright hues, there the brilliant novelty of the scene, that strange beauty to which the eye never becomes wholly accustomed, would seem to arouse the fancy to unusual activity. Images, quaint and strange, rise unbidden and fill the mind, until we pause at length to make sure that, amid the novel aspect of the country, its inhabitants are still the same; we look again to convince ourselves that the pillared cottages, the wooden churches, the brick trading-houses, the long and many-windowed taverns, are still what they were a month earlier.

The softening haze of the Indian summer, so common at the same season, adds to the illusory character of the view. The mountains have grown higher; their massive forms have acquired a new dignity from the airy veil which enfolds them, just as the drapery of ancient marbles serves to give additional grace to the movement of a limb, or to mark more nobly the proportions of the form over which it is thrown. The different ridges, the lesser knolls, rise before us with new importance; the distances of the perspective are magnified; and yet, at the same time, the comparative relations which the different objects bear to each other, are revealed with a beautiful accuracy wanting in a clearer atmosphere, where the unaided eye is more apt to err.

There is always something of uncertainty, of caprice if you will, connected with our American autumn, which fixes the attention anew, every succeeding year, and adds to the fanciful character of the season. The beauty of spring is of a more assured nature; the same tints rise year after year in her verdure, and in her blossoms, but autumn is what our friends in France call *"une beauté journalière,"* variable, changeable, not alike twice in succession, gay and brilliant yesterday, more languid and pale to-day. The hill-sides, the different groves, the single trees, vary from year to year under the combined influences of clouds and sunshine, the soft haze, or the clear frost; the maple or oak, which last October was gorgeous crimson, may choose this season to wear the golden tint of the chestnut, or the pale yellow of duller trees; the ash, which was straw-color, may become dark purple. One never knows beforehand exactly what to expect; there is always some variation, occasionally a strange contrast. It is like awaiting the sunset of a brilliant day; we feel confident that the evening sky will be beautiful, but what gorgeous clouds or what pearly tints may appear to delight the eye, no one can foretell.

It was a soft hazy morning, early in October. The distant hills, with their rounded, dome-like heights, rising in every direction, had assumed on the surface of their crowning woods a rich tint of bronze, as though the swelling summits, gleaming in the sunlight, were wrought in fretted ornaments of that metal. Here and there a scarlet maple stood in full colored beauty, amid surrounding groves of green. A group of young oaks close at hand had also felt the influence of the frosty autumnal dews; their foliage, generally, was a lively green, worthy of June, wholly unlike decay, and yet each tree was touched here and there with vivid snatches of the brightest red; the smaller twigs close to the trunk forming brilliant crimson tufts, like knots of ribbon. One might have fancied them a band of young knights, wearing their ladies' colors over their hearts. A pretty flowering dogwood close at hand, with delicate shaft and airy branches, flushed with its own peculiar tint of richest lake, was perchance the lady of the grove, the beauty whose colors were fluttering on the breasts of the knightly oaks on either side. The tiny seedling maples, with their delicate leaflets, were also in color, in choice shades of scarlet, crimson, and pink, like a new race of flowers blooming about the roots of the autumnal forest.

We were sitting upon the trunk of a fallen pine, near a projecting cliff which overlooked the country for some fifteen miles or more; the lake, the rural town, and the farms in the valley beyond, lying at our feet like a beautiful map. A noisy flock of blue-jays were chattering among the oaks whose branches overshadowed our seat, and a busy squirrel was dropping his winter store of chestnuts from another tree close at hand. A gentle breeze from the south came rustling through the colored woods, and already there was an autumnal sound in their murmurs. There is a difference in the music of the woods as the seasons change. In winter, when the waving limbs are bare, there is more of unity in the deep wail of the winds as they sweep through the forests; in summer the rustling foliage gives some higher and more cheerful notes to the general harmony; and there is also a change of key from the softer murmurs of the fresh foliage of early summer, to the sharp tones of the dry and withering leaves in October.

There is something of a social spirit in the brilliancy of our American autumn. All the glory of the colored forest would seem displayed for human eyes to enjoy; there is, in its earlier stages, an air of festive gayety which accords well with the cheerful labors of the season, and there is a richness in the spectacle worthy of the harvest-home of a fruitful land. I should not care to pass the season in the wilderness which still covers large portions of the country; either winter or summer should be the time for roaming in those boundless woods; but with October let us return to a peopled region. A broad extent of forest is no doubt necessary to the magnificent spectacle, but there should also be broken woods, scattered groves, and isolated trees; and it strikes me that the quiet fields of man, and his cheerful dwellings, should also have a place in the gay picture. Yes; we felt convinced that an autumn view of the valley at our feet must be finer in its present varied aspect, than in past ages when wholly covered with wood.

The hand of man generally improves a landscape. The earth has been given to him, and his presence in Eden is natural; he gives life and spirit to the garden. It is only when he endeavors to rise above his true part of laborer and husbandman, when he assumes the character of creator, and piles you up hills, pumps you up a river, scatters stones, or sprinkles cascades, that he is apt to fail. Generally the grassy meadow in the valley, the winding road climbing the hill-side, the cheerful village on the bank of the stream, give a higher additional interest to the view; or where there is something amiss in the scene, it is when there is some evident want of judgment, or good sense, or perhaps some proof of selfish avarice, or wastefulness, as when a country is stripped of its wood to fill the pockets or feed the fires of one generation.

It is true there are scenes on so vast a scale, scenes so striking in themselves, that whatever there may be of man in view is at first wholly overlooked; we note the valley, but not his villages; we see the winding stream, but not the fisher's skiff; even in these instances, however, after the first vivid impressions produced by the grandeur of the spectacle, we please ourselves by dwelling on the lesser features awhile; and after wondering on the Righi-Kulm at the sublime array of hoary Alps bounding the distant horizon, we pause to note the smoke curling from the hamlet in the nearest valley, we mark the châlets dotting the mountain-side, or the white sail of the boat making its way across the lake.

Even in those sublime scenes, where no trace of man meets the eye, in the cheerless monotony of the steppes of central Asia, in the arid deserts of Africa, among the uninhabited Andes, or in the boundless forests of America, it is the absence of human life which is so highly impressive; and if other portions of the earth were not peopled with intellectual beings, mapped out by them and marked with their works, the contrast of those strange solitudes could not be felt by the heart of the wanderer.

All the other innumerable tribes of animated beings inhabiting this world, may crowd a country, and scarcely make an impression on its face which the winds and rains of a few seasons will not wholly obliterate; but man, in his most savage condition, shall raise some fortification, or heap over the bones of his heroes some vast misshapen pile, which outlasts perhaps the existence of a whole race. The southeastern portion of Europe is a vast level region, resembling in many particulars the steppes of central Asia, or the great prairies of our own country; until recently it lay a broad unpeopled waste, no part of which had been brought under cultivation; but in the midst of these grassy solitudes rise rude ancient tumuli, or barrows, whose origin goes back to periods anterior to history; nomadic shepherd tribes passed and repassed the ground for ages, but knew nothing of their story. Similar tumuli are numerous in western Asia also, and, like the mounds of our own continent, they doubtless belong to a rude and ancient race. These old works of earth, whose great piles refuse to reveal the names of those who reared them, never fail to excite a peculiar interest; there is a spirit of mystery hovering over them beyond what is connected with monuments of any later period, even the proudest labors in stone; so like the works of nature in this respect, they seem to possess for us something of the same profound secrecy. These lasting and remarkable tumuli, or mounds, although they produce no very striking effect on the aspect of a country, yet have an important place in the long array of works which give a peculiar character to the lands which man has once held as his own.

The monuments of a succeeding age, raised by a more skilful people, are much more prominent. Indeed it would seem as if man had no sooner mastered the art of architecture, than he aimed at rivalling the dignity and durability of the works of nature which served as his models; he resolved that his walls of vast stones should stand in place as long as the rocks from which they were hewn; that his columns and his arches should live with the trees and branches from which they were copied; he determined to scale the heavens with his proud towers of Babel. The durability of their architecture still remains to the present day one of the most remarkable characteristics of those ancient ages. Such is the wonder excited in the minds of the most skilful architects of the present day at the sight of the immense masses of stone transported and uplifted, apparently at will, by those ancient nations, that some have supposed them to have possessed mechanical powers of their own, lost to succeeding ages, and not yet regained by ourselves. Certainly it would appear a well-assured fact, that the oldest works of the first great architects have been the most enduring and the most imposing of all that human art has raised. How many centuries were required to ruin Babylon! With the prophetic curse of desolation hovering over her towers for ages, the violence of a dozen generations was aroused against her, nation after nation was brought to the work, ere that curse was fulfilled, and all her pride laid in the dust; and still to-day her shapeless ruins break the surface of the level desert which surrounds them. Look at the ancient temples of India; look at Egypt with her wonderful works; all the proudest edifices of modern times may yet fall to the ground, ere those Pyramids are ruined; they may see the last future acts of the earth's story, as they have stood mute witnesses of a thousand past histories. What were that level country of Egypt, that muddy Nile, without the Pyramids and the surrounding coeval monuments!

Look, even later, at the works of Grecian and Roman art. Although Greece and Rome were the chosen prey of barbarous nations for ages, yet not all the fury of millions of savages could utterly destroy the monuments they raised. Study the ruined temples, and theatres, and tombs, the aqueducts, the bridges of those ancient nations. What architectural labors have we which for excellence and beauty will compare with them? For thousands of years they have stood, noble, distinctive features of the lands to which they belong. The little temple of the Sybil seems, to modern eyes, as much an integral part of the surrounding hills, and the valley of Tivoli, as the evergreen oaks and olive trees, ay, as the stream which flings itself over the rocks at its feet. What were the Campagna, without its broken aqueducts, its ancient tombs? What were Rome itself without its ruins? The architectural

human progress
adding to natural
world

remains of those old works still give to the seven hills, and the broad
plain about them, a positive beauty, which their modern works, imposing as they are, cannot equal.

It is well for us that those races of old undertook such noble labors.
May we not believe that there was something Providential in the feeling which led them to erect such lasting monuments? They built for
us. Such works as the Pyramids, and their cotemporary temples, such
works as those of Babel, Pæstum, the Coliseum, the Parthenon, belong to the race; their influence is not confined to the soil on which
they stand. As the sun of Time descends to complete its course, their
shadows are thrown over the whole earth.

In the middle ages, after Europe had become Christian, all the edifices of sufficient importance to give character to a country were divided in two great classes; they were the Gothic churches and abbeys
of religion, or the fortified castles of war. It is rather singular that the
age of the greatest extent of religious houses should also have been
peculiarly an age of warfare; but no doubt the very prevalence of this
warlike spirit was a cause of the increase of monarchism. If the dozen
hills about a valley were each crowned with a castle, and if half a dozen
feuds between their different lords laid waste the surrounding country,
it became a sort of necessity for a Christian society that one house of
peace, at least, should lie in the meadows of the valley, in view from the
towers. The very violence of the age, united to the superstitious nature
of religion at the time, was thus no doubt a cause of the great size and
riches of the churches. Louis XI. of France, as a general rule, commit-
ted some act of cruelty or treachery every morning, and then sought
to buy a pardon in the evening by some pecuniary favor to church or
abbey; and there were in those days many knights and barons bold
whose consciences were appeased by the same course of proceeding.

The durability of the works of the middle ages—although they had
lost so much of ancient civilization—is still very remarkable. Some of
the cathedrals, the castles, and the bridges of those days are likely, with
a few exceptions here and there, to outlast modern works of the same

nature; certainly they may outlast those now standing in this country. There are bridges of that period in the wildest parts of Europe, so bold in their position, spanning gorges so deep, springing from precipices so abrupt, that the people of later days gave them a magical origin, calling them "Devils' Bridges." There are feudal castles with walls so massive, that the idea of razing them was abandoned after the orders to do so had been given. Their vast cathedrals, whose noble spires still rise so grandly above the roofs of the towns to which they belong, were ages in building; some of these, nay, one may say many of them, required such vast sums of money, and such a long period of time to carry out the great designs of their architects, that they have remained unfinished to the present hour. They not only built for the future, in those days, but they expected posterity to work with them; and as one generation lay down in their graves, they called another generation to the pious labor.

It is not exactly as a stranger that an American looks at these remains of feudal days, that he stands before the half-ruined walls of their castles; in one sense we also have an interest in them. Who knows but ancestors of our own may have been among the squires who crossed that drawbridge, or among the masons who built the walls, or with the peasants who clustered under the protection of the banners of yonder ruined hold? At any rate there is no one breathing in Christendom whose present fate, perhaps both for good and for evil, has not been in some measure influenced by those days of chivalry and superstitious truth, in their bearing upon civilized society at large. We Americans are as much the children of those European ages, as the present population of France or England.

The vast extent of the regions over which these ancient monuments are scattered, the different series of them on the same soil—Druidical, Roman, Gothic, Renaissance and modern—give one a clearer idea than figures can, of the innumerable throngs of human beings which have preceded the present tenants of the ground, and so fully stamped the impression of man on the face of the old world. The plains, the hills, the valleys, the cliffs, the bare and massive mountains, the islands, the very caves of those regions, all bear ancient human marks. The plains are crowned by remains of Roman roads; the valleys and the islands have been the seat of old monasteries, or perhaps still older villas; the hills, the cliffs, the mountains, are crowned with the ruined towers of feudal days; the wild gorges and the caves have been the haunts of banded robbers and outlaws, or of solitary hermits.

The caves of the old world, more especially those of the eastern and southern countries, of Syria, Arabia, Egypt, Greece, Italy, have had a strange story of their own. Many of them have been strongholds, which have stood siege after siege, as for instance those of Palestine and Egypt. Others have been the dens of robbers, or pirates. Many, cut in the face of high and apparently inaccessible cliffs, have been used as tombs, and are more or less carved and sculptured within and without; such are frequently seen in Syria and other parts of Asia. In southern Italy there are many caves in the face of the cliffs of the Apennines, whose openings are plainly seen from the highways in the valleys below; those were at one time, when Italy was overrun by barbarous heathen nations, the refuge of Christian hermits. Probably the natural caves of those Eastern lands were the first dwellings of their earliest population. Thus it is that there is not in those old countries a single natural feature of the earth upon which man has not set his seal, from the cave of Machpelah to the summit of the Alpine mountain, where the pale gray lines of the distant cross are faintly drawn against the sky.

How different from all this is the aspect of our own country! It is true that our fathers, with amazing rapidity, have changed a forest wilderness into a civilized and populous land. But the fresh civilization of America is wholly different in aspect from that of the old world; there is no blending of the old and the new in this country; there is nothing old among us. If we were endowed with ruins we should not preserve them; they would be pulled down to make way for some novelty. A striking instance of this tendency will be found in the fact that

the last Dutch house in New-York has disappeared. For a long time a
number of those historical way-marks existed in the older parts of the
town, but now, we understand that the last high gable, the last Dutch
walls, have disappeared from New Amsterdam. We might have supposed that occupying so little space as they did, standing in streets
with Dutch names, owned perhaps by men of Dutch descent, one, at
least, of these relics of our own olden time might have been preserved.
But no; we are the reverse of conservators in this country; it was idle
perhaps to expect that a single monument of the origin of the town
would be left in place.

  We are the borderers of civilization in America, but borderers of the
nineteenth century, when all distances are lessened, whether moral or
physical. And then, as borderers, we also often act as pioneers; the
peculiar tendencies of the age are seen more clearly among us than in
Europe. The civilization of the present is far more subtle in its character than that of the past, and its works are naturally like itself, highly
influential, and important, but less dignified, and imposing in aspect.
It would be comparatively an easy work to remove from the earth all
traces of many of the peculiar merits of modern civilization, just as
the grand Palace of Glass, now standing in London, that brilliant and
characteristic work of the day, might in a few hours be utterly razed.
Look at our light suspension bridges, marvellous as they are, how soon
they could be destroyed; look at our railways, at our ships and man-
ufactories moved by steam; look at the marvellous electric telegraph,
at the wonders Daguerre has showed us—look, in fact, at any of the
peculiar and most remarkable of the works of the age, and see how
speedily all traces of them could be removed. It will be said that the
most important of all arts, that of printing, must suffice in itself to preserve all other discoveries: assuredly; but remove the art of printing,
bring fresh hordes of barbarians to sweep over the civilized world, let
them busy themselves with the task of destruction, and say then what
traces of our works would remain on the face of the earth as monuments of our period. Perchance, as regards America, the chief proofs

that eastern civilization had once passed over this country would then be found in the mingled vegetation, the trees, the plants, ay, the very weeds of the old world.

We are told by Monsieur Agassiz that, as the surface of the planet now exists, North America is, in reality, the oldest part of the earth. He tells us that in many particulars our vegetation, and our animal life, belong to an older period than those of the eastern hemisphere; he tells us of fossil hickories, and fossil gar-pikes in Europe, while hickories and gar-pikes are now confined to our own part of the world. But without doubting this theory, still there are many peculiarities which give to this country an air of youth beyond what is observed in the East. There are many parts of Europe, of Asia, of Africa, which have an old, worn-out, exhausted appearance; sterile mountains, unwooded moors, barren deserts and plains. In North America, on the contrary, there is little territory which can be called really sterile. As a general rule, the extent and richness of its forests and its wealth of waters give it naturally a cheerful aspect, while the more rounded forms of the hills and mountains, and their covering of vegetation, leave an impression of youth on the mind, compared with the abrupt, rocky peaks, the smaller streams, and the open unwooded plains of eastern regions.

The comparatively slight and fugitive character of American architecture, no doubt, gives additional force to this impression. Seldom indeed are our edifices imposing. The chief merit of our masonry and carpentry, especially when taken in the mass, where the details are not critically examined, is a pleasing character of cheerfulness. It is not the airy elegance of French or Italian art; it is not the gayety of the Moorish or Arabesque; it is yet too unformed, too undecided to claim a character of its own, but the general air of comfort and thrift which shows itself in most of our dwellings, whether on a large or a small scale, gives satisfaction in its way.

Such were the thoughts which came to us as we sat on the fallen pine, among the October woods, overlooking the country. Before bending our steps homeward we amused ourselves with a sort of game

of architectural consequences, the result of the preceding fancies. I
had gathered a sprig of wych-hazel, and, waving it over the valley,
determined to make a trial of its well-established magical powers. No
sooner had the forked branch, garnished with its ragged yellow flowers, been waved to and fro, than strange work began! The wooden
bridge at the entrance of the village fell into the stream and disappeared; the court-house vanished; the seven taverns were gone; the
dozen stores had felt the spell; the churches were not spared; the hundred dwelling-houses shared the same fate, and vanished like the
smoke from their own chimneys. Merely razing a village was not,
however, our ambition; so we again had recourse to the leafless twig of
wych-hazel. Scarcely had it passed once more over the valley, when we
saw a forest start from the earth, the trees in full maturity, of the same
variety of species, and in the same stage of autumnal coloring with
the woods about us. But even this reappearance of a forest on the site
of the vanished village did not satisfy the whim of the moment. The
branch of wych-hazel was again rapidly waved towards the four quar-
ters of the heavens, and so great was the agitation of the movement,
that a number of its yellow ragged petals were broken off, and scattered by the wind over the country. Perhaps the blossoms increased
the power of the spell, for in another moment we beheld a spectacle
which wholly engrossed our attention. We had been indulging in the
wish to have a view of the valley in the condition it would have assumed, had it lain in the track of European civilization during past
ages; how, in such a case, would it have been fashioned by the hand of
man? To our amazement the wish was now granted. But it required a
second close scrutiny to convince us that this was indeed the site of the
village which had disappeared a moment earlier, every thing was so
strangely altered. We soon convinced ourselves, however, that all the
natural features of the landscape remained precisely as we had always
known them; not a curve in the outline of the lake was changed, not
a knoll was misplaced. The vegetation was such as we had long been
familiar with, and the coloring of the autumnal woods precisely what

it had been an hour earlier. But here all resemblance ceased. Many of
the hills had been wholly shorn of wood. The position of the different
farms and that of the buildings was entirely changed. Looking down
upon the little town we saw it had dwindled to a mere hamlet; low,
picturesque, thatched cottages were irregularly grouped along a wide
grassy street, and about a broad green which formed the centre of the
village; in this open grassy green stood a large stone cross, beautifully
designed and elaborately carved, doubtless a monument of some past
historical event. One small inn, the only tavern, faced the green and
the cross, and a large sign swung heavily before the door. The church,
the largest building in the hamlet, was evidently very old, and covered a good deal of ground—its walls were low, of hewn stone—one
large and rich window occupied the eastern end, and a graceful spire
rose in the opposite direction. Two or three small, quiet-looking shops
represented the trade of the place. The bridge was of massive stone,
narrow, and highly arched, while the ruins of a tower stood close at
hand. The fields were parted by hedges, which lined the narrow roads
on either side. Several country houses were seen in the neighborhood,
in various grades of importance. There was a pretty thatched cottage,
with one large bay window for front, and surrounded by a gay flower-
garden. Then just without the village was a place of some size, evidently an old country house, dating perhaps some six or eight generations back, with its brick walls, quaint chimneys, angles, cornices, and
additions; this place could boast its park, and deer were grazing on the
lawn. Yonder in the distance, upon the western shore of the lake, stood
a castle of gray stone, its half dozen towers rising a hundred feet from
the hill-side; there were beautiful lawns and broad masses of wood in
this extensive domain; the building itself was in good condition, and
apparently inhabited. On a pretty point, projecting into the lake about
a league from the village, stood a half-ruined convent, now reduced
to a mere farm-house. Something whispered to us that a Roman road
had once passed in that direction, that a villa had formerly stood on the
same spot as the Priory, and that ancient coins were occasionally dug

up there. The modern highways running through the valley were the most perfect that can be conceived. No less than nine different hamlets were in sight from our position on the cliff; two, in addition to the village at our feet, were seated on the lake shore; three more were seen clinging to the hill-sides, grouped about sites where feudal castles had stood in former times; another appeared on the bank of the river, at a point long used as a ford, and two more occupied different positions in the valley. Pretty gray spires, or low church towers, were seen rising above most of these hamlets. On the farthest hill to the northward, and from its highest point, the ruins of an ancient watchtower rose above the wood.

I could carry my observations no further. The yellow flowers of the wych-hazel in my hand had attracted a roving bee, bent apparently on improving these last warm days, and harvesting the last drops of honey; the little creature had crept close to a finger, and a sharp sting soon recalled my wandering attention, and caused me to drop the branch and the bee together. The magic wych-hazel thrown aside, the spell was over; the country had resumed its every-day aspect.

Introduction to John Leonard Knapp's
Country Rambles in England;
or, Journal of a Naturalist

IT IS NOW nearly five-and-twenty years since the "Journal of a Naturalist" first appeared in England. The author, Mr. Knapp, has told us himself that the book owes its origin to the "Natural History of Selborne," a work of the last century, which it is quite needless to say has become one of the standards of English literature; and the reader is probably also aware that the honors acceded to the disciple are, in this instance, scarcely less than those of his master—the "Journal of a Naturalist," and "Selborne," stand side by side, on the same shelf, in the better libraries of England.

Both volumes belong to a choice class; they are to be numbered among the books which have been written neither for fame nor for profit, but which have opened spontaneously, one might almost say unconsciously, from the author's mind. The subjects on which they touch are such as must always prove interesting in themselves; like the grass of the field, and the trees of the wood, the growth of both works has been fostered by the showers and the sunshine of the open heavens; and in spite of so much that is artificial in our daily life and habits, there are hours when all our hearts gladly turn to the natural and unperverted gifts of our Maker.

"The History of Selborne," and the "Journal of a Naturalist," happen to have been both written in the southern counties of England. Selborne, the parish of which the Rev. Gilbert White was Rector, lies on the eastern borders of Hampshire. Mr. Knapp has not given us the

name of his own village; but its position in Gloucestershire is minutely
described. He tells us that it stands upon a high ridge of land com-
manding very beautiful views, including the broad estuary of the Severn, and the rich plains on its banks, while the fine mountains of southern Wales fill up the back-ground; a Roman ferry with the sites of
ancient stations, and the lines of old roads of the same people, are visible, and the pretty though unimportant town of Thornbury, with its
imposing church and castle, occupy the cliffs on the opposite bank of
the river.

"The smooth Severn stream,"

with its

"Rush-yfringed bank
Where grows the willow, and the osier dank,"

is the only river of any size in England, running north and south. It
rises in Wales, at the foot of Plinlimmon, and winding through some
of the finest plains on the island, waters the towns of Shrewsbury,
Worcester, Tewksbury, and Gloucester. How familiar are all these
names to American ears; how the scroll of history unfolds before the
mind's eye as we read their titles! During the last century the importance of the Severn, in a commercial sense, was very great indeed;
the movement on the broad estuary by which it flows into the ocean,
being perhaps greater, at that period, than that of any other European
river, with the single exception of the Thames. Many have been the
naval expeditions of importance which have sailed from the Severn;
the Cabots when bound on the daring voyage which first threw the
light of civilization upon the coast of North America, embarked from
the wharves of Bristol. Perchance the scanty sails, and heavy hull of
their craft, as it made its way sea-ward, may have been watched by
some wondering peasant, toiling in the same fields to which the Naturalist has introduced us.

The mountains of Wales, filling the back-ground of the picture sketched in the author's opening pages, are very different from those with which American eyes are familiar. Bare and bleak, they are usually wholly shorn of wood, and far bolder in their craggy outline than our own heights. Snowdon, the most important mountain in Wales, rises to a height of 3700 feet. Standing in a northern county of the Principality it is not, however, to be included in a view from the banks of the southern Severn. But the hills of Glamorgan, and Brecon, especially noticed by Mr. Knapp, are upward of 2000 feet in height, and stamped more or less with the same general character. It often happens indeed, from the boldness of position, and the abruptness of outline, which usually mark the mountains of Europe, that heights of no great elevation produce very striking effects in a view.

The fertile alluvial pastures in the immediate foreground of the picture, are those in which Milton's river-nymph Sabrina, may be supposed to have strayed:

> "Still she retains
> Her maiden gentleness, and oft at eve
> Visits the herds along the twilight meadows,
> Helping all urchin blasts, and ill-luck signs
> That the shrewd meddling elf delights to make,
> Which she with precious vial'd liquors heals;
> For which the shepherds at their festivals
> Carol her goodness loud in rustic lays,
> And throw sweet garland wreaths into her stream
> Of pansies, pinks, and gaudy daffodils."

The little village, the immediate scene of the Naturalist's observations, appears to have had an uneventful existence. It lies, we are told, "on a very ancient road," running between the cities of Gloucester and Bristol; doubtless the tide of war and adventure, must often have swept over the track on many occasions, when the interests of England were battled for in the western counties of the kingdom, but only scanty vestiges of its passage have been found in the little community. A few skeletons, accidentally dug up by the road-side, the bones of horses, the iron head of a single lance, are alone alluded to as memorials of some nameless conflict of the period of Cromwell, and his wars. No stern feudal towers, no ambitious monastic edifices appear to have been raised within the limits of the parish; and, in short, the position of the spot is one associated chiefly with simple rustic labors, and rural quiet, a field especially in harmony with the inquiries and pursuits of the lover of nature.

It is with the vegetation of this unambitious region, and with the living creatures by which it is peopled, that the Naturalist would make us acquainted. He tells us of the trees found in the groves and copses of that open country; of the grasses which grow in the meadows on the banks of the Severn; of the grains and plants cultivated in the hedged fields which line his ancient road. He has a great deal to say about the birds which fly to and fro, with the passing seasons; about the butter-flies, and moths which come and go with the summer blossoms, and he is familiar with the lowliest of the creeping things found upon his path. Such simple lore is never without interest to those who delight in the face of the earth, to those who love to honor the Creator in the study of his works. It is pleasant to know familiarly the plants which spring up at our feet; we like to establish a sort of intimacy with the birds which, year after year, come singing about our homes; and, on the other hand, when told of the wonders of a foreign vegetation, differing essentially from our own, when hearing of the habits of strange creatures from other and distant climates, we listen eagerly as to a tale of novelty.

We Americans, indeed, are peculiarly placed in this respect. As a people, we are still, in some sense, half aliens to the country Providence has given us; there is much ignorance among us regarding the creatures which held the land as their own long before our forefathers trod the soil, and many of which are still moving about us, living accessories of our existence, at the present hour. On the other hand,

again, English reading has made us very familiar with the names, at
least, of those races which people the old world. From the nursery
epic, relating the melancholy fate of "Cock Robin," and the numerous feathered *dramatis personæ* figuring in its verses; from the tragical
histories of "Little Red Riding Hood," and the "Babes in the Woods;"
from the winged and four-footed company of Gay and Lafontaine,
from these associates of our childhood to the larks and nightingales
of Shakspeare and Milton, we all, as we move from the nursery to the
library, gather notions more or less definite. We fancy that we know all
these creatures by sight; and yet neither "Cock Robin," nor his mur-
derer the Sparrow, nor his parson the Rook, is to be found this side the
salt sea; the cunning Wolf whose hypocritical personation of the old
grandame, so wrung our little hearts once upon a time, is not the wolf
which howled only a few years since in the forests our fathers felled;
the wily Fox of Lafontaine,

> "Certain renard Gascon,
> D'autres disent Normand,"

is not the fox of Yankeeland—albeit we have our foxes too! Neither
the Marten,

> "The temple-loving martlet, does approve
> By his lov'd mansioning that the heavens breath
> Smells wooingly here. * * *
> where they
> "Most breed, and haunt, I have observed the air
> Is delicate;"

nor the nightingale who

> "Sings darkling, and in the shadiest covert hid,
> Tunes her nocturnal notes;"

nor the lark

> "The herald of the morn,"

flies within three thousand miles of our own haunts. Thus it is that knowing so little of the creatures in whose midst we live, and mentally familiar by our daily reading with the tribes of another hemisphere, the forms of one continent and the names and characters of another, are strangely blended in most American minds. And in this dream-like phantasmagoria, where fancy and reality are often so widely at variance, in which the objects we see, and those we read of are wholly different, and where bird and beast undergo metamorphoses so strange, most of us are content to pass through life.

But there is a pleasant task awaiting us. We may all, if we choose, open our eyes to the beautiful and wonderful realities of the world we live in. Why should we any longer walk blindfold through the fields? Americans, we repeat, are peculiarly placed in this respect; the nature of both hemispheres lies open before them, that of the old world having all the charm of traditional association to attract their attention, that of their native soil being endued with the still deeper interest of home affections. The very comparison between the two is a subject full of the highest interest, a subject more than sufficing in itself to provide instruction and entertainment for a lifetime. And yet, how many of us are ignorant of the very striking, leading fact that the indigenous races of both hemispheres, whether vegetable or animal, while they are generally more or less nearly related to each other, are rarely indeed identical. The number of individual plants, or birds, or insects, which are precisely similar in both hemispheres, is surprisingly small.

It will probably be unnecessary to observe that the writer of these remarks must be understood as laying no claim to the honorable position of a teacher, on either of the many branches connected with Natural History; a mere learner herself, she can offer the reader no other guidance than that of companionship, in looking after the birds, or plants, or insects, mentioned by Mr. Knapp. It has indeed been a subject of regret with her, that the task of editing the "Journal of a Naturalist" should not have fallen into hands better able to render the author full justice in this respect. But it is the object of the present edition to prepare this English volume for the American public generally, and for that purpose simple explanations were alone necessary. Anxious, at least, to do all in her power, the editor has consulted the best printed authorities within her reach, and she has also availed herself of the valuable and most obliging assistance of Professor S. F. Baird, Major Le Conte, and Mr. M. A. Curtis, while preparing several of the notes, which will be found in the appendix.

S. F. C.

August, 1852.

Introduction to
The Rhyme and Reason of Country Life:
Or, Selections from Fields
Old and New

Passive Voice

THE ANCIENT classical writers of the world are thought to have shown but little sensibility to that natural beauty with which the earth has been clothed, as with a magnificent garment, by her Almighty Creator. Those of their works which have been preserved to us are declared by critics rarely to bear evidence of much depth of feeling of this kind. The German scholars are understood to have been the first to broach this opinion—the first to point out the fact, and to comment on what appears a singular inconsistency.

"If we bear in mind," says Schiller, "the beautiful scenery with which the Greeks were surrounded, and remember the opportunities possessed by a people living in so genial a climate, of entering into the free enjoyment of the contemplation of nature, and observe how conformable were their mode of thought, the bent of their imaginations, and the habits of their lives to the simplicity of nature, which was so faithfully reflected in their poetic works, we can not fail to remark with surprise how few traces are to be met among them of the sentimental interest with which we in modern times attach ourselves to the individual characteristics of natural scenery. The Greek poet is certainly in the highest degree correct, faithful, and circumstantial in his descriptions of nature, but his heart has no more share in his words than if he were treating of a garment, a shield, or a suit of armor. Nature seems to interest his understanding more than his moral perceptions; he does not cling to her charms with the fervor and the plaintive passion of the poet of modern times."

This passage of Schiller, quoted in "Cosmos," is supported by similar observations of M. de Humboldt himself: "Specific descriptions of nature occur only as accessories, for in Grecian art all things are centered in the sphere of human life." And, again: "The description of nature in its manifold richness of form, as a distinct branch of poetic literature, was wholly unknown to the Greeks. The landscape appears among them merely as the background of the picture, of which human figures constitute the main subject." Touches of description must of course occasionally occur, and whenever these are found, the harmony of Grecian taste gives them the highest beauty possible. The many noble similes and comparisons scattered through the greater poems, form admirable detached pictures; but they occupy the attention very briefly; a rapid glance is thrown upon the hill, the river, or the wood, rather for the purpose of affording greater relief to the figures in the foreground than of enduing the sketch of these features of the earth with any charm or importance in itself. But it is quite impossible to believe for a moment that the Greeks, so fully alive to the spirit of beauty in all its other forms, should have been blind to its effects in the natural world. Other ways of accounting for the apparent inconsistency must be sought for, and the peculiar character and position of the people would seem to suggest these. It was quite consistent with the condition of the world at that early period, and of the Greeks in particular, that nature and art should not then hold the same relative places which they occupy to-day. Art was still in its youth, and of more importance to them than it is to us. Nature, with all her untold wealth, her unharvested magnificence, lay before them, close at hand, always within reach; there was no fear that she should fail them. But human Art was in its earliest stages of culture; every successive step was watched with most lively interest; every progressive movement became of great importance, while the genius of the Greeks particularly led them to feel extreme delight in every achievement of the kind. In fact, all their highest enjoyments flowed from this source, and into this sphere they threw themselves with their whole soul. Whatever susceptibility to the grandeur and beauty of the inanimate creation was felt among them, sought therefore rather to express itself in forms more positive than the voice of song. What, for instance, was the most noble of their temples but the image in Dorian marble of some grand primeval grove, whose gray, columnar trunks they found reflected in the waves of the Ægean Sea? What were the vase, and the vine wreathed about its lip, but the repetition of living forms of fruits and foliage growing in the vale of Tempe, or at the foot of Hymettus? The Greek mind thus beheld the whole external world chiefly through the medium of human Art. An interesting and very striking instance of this peculiarity occurs in the Iliad; no natural object which has a place in the poem—neither the sea nor the skies, neither the streams nor the mountains, all glowing as these were with the purple light of a Grecian atmosphere—could draw from Homer a description filling half the space allotted by him to the shield of Achilles; nay, more, observe that where rural life and its accessories appear the most distinctly in his verse, it is not the reality which he shows us; we do not ourselves tread the brown soil of the freshly-tilled fallow; we do not pass along the one narrow path in the vineyard, amid the purple clusters, but we are called upon to behold these objects—"sight to be admired of all!"—as they lie curiously graven by the hand of Vulcan on the bronze buckler of the hero, where he

> * * * "With devices multiform, the disk
> Capacious charged, toiling with skill divine."

Their very religion was but a work of art, a brilliant web of the human imagination, into which, as on the metal of Vulcan, their poets had wrought

> "Borders beauteous, dazzling bright,"

where Olympic deities passed to and fro, with grace and spirit unequaled, but moving ever by the springs of the most common of human passions. All the inanimate objects of the visible creation had their allotted places in this gorgeous, imaginative tissue, though still appearing under associations purely human. They had, in short, no conceptions of nature independent of man; to them the whole world was but the shield of Achilles.

With the same mythology, the same philosophy as the Greeks, the Romans are admitted to have been essentially plagiarists. They saw the earth, in this sense, with the eyes of the Greeks. Their literature has even been accused of a greater dearth of poetical observation, as regards the natural world, than that of their predecessors. The practical realities of life engrossed their attention more exclusively. A colossal selfishness was their striking national characteristic—a characteristic which was alike the cause, first, of their political prosperity, and later of their downfall. Rome was their deity; to her daily needs, or interests, or pleasures, all was sacrificed; they cared little for the mountains, and forests, and streams of the earth, provided all the wealth and magnificence of these were brought over Roman ways to swell the triumph of the Forum. It has been remarked that Cæsar could pass the Alps, then comparatively an unknown region, without one allusion to their sublime character. Still, a body of men like the great Latin writers could not, of course, exist devoid of susceptibility to the beauty of the inanimate world, and many passages may be drawn from their poems bearing witness to this fact. Although, says M. de Humboldt, there is no individual rural portraiture in the Æneid, yet "a deep and intimate comprehension of nature is depicted in soft colors. Where, for instance, has the gentle play of the waves, or the stillness of night, been more happily described?" The modern reader, however, is still left to wonder that poets so great should not have delighted more frequently in enlarging upon similar topics, and that even in many of their elegiac works social life should so exclusively fill up the space.[1] We should have rather supposed that when the earth stood in her primitive freshness, in the morning of her existence, her wealth of beauty as yet unsung, that the works of the first great poets would have been filled with the simple reflection of her natural glory. But, as we have seen, such was not the case with the writers of Greece or of Rome; and, as we have already ventured to intimate, it would appear that the great intellectual activity of those races, connected with the period of time filled by them, where so wide a field opened in every direction, became in itself a prominent cause of this peculiar deficiency of their literature. Whatever admiration they felt for nature expressed itself in positive forms of art, or in an imaginative system of mythology, rather than in song.

But something of a different spirit appears to have actuated the old Asiatic nations. The ancient Indian races, for instance, were more contemplative in character, and more vivid impressions of natural objects are revealed in their writings. The Sanscrit Hymns, and the heroic poems of the same language, are said to contain fine descriptive passages. "The main subject of these writings," says M. de Humboldt, speaking of the Sanscrit Vedas, "is the veneration and praise of Nature." A poem, called "The Seasons"—and one starts at the familiar name—with another work, called "The Messenger of the Clouds," are full, we are told, of the same spirit; they were written by Kalidasa, a cotemporary of Virgil and Horace. It would have given us pleasure to offer the reader a few fragments from writings so ancient and so interesting; one would have liked to compare a passage from the Sanscrit Seasons with those so celebrated and so familiar from our own language and modern time, but no English versions are found within reach. The fact, however, of this characteristic of the Sanscrit poems is placed beyond reasonable doubt by the declarations of many distinguished men of learning, more particularly among the German scholars.

The Chinese, that singular people which for ages have separated themselves from the rest of the earth by impassable barriers of prejudice and mystery, are now found—as glimpses are opening into their interior—to have long shown some partiality for natural beauty. Among other poems, touching more or less upon subjects of this kind, they have one bearing the simple name of "The Garden," which was written by See-ma-kuang, a celebrated statesman, some eight or nine centuries since, and which is said to contain agreeable descriptive passages; the sketch of a hermitage among rocks and evergreen woods, and a fine, extensive water view over one of their great rivers, are especially referred to. Lieu-schew, another ancient writer of theirs, dwells at length on the subject of pleasure-grounds, for which he gives admirable directions, in the English style, at a period when a really fine garden was not to be found in all Northern Europe; a short translation from a passage of his will be found in the following selections. Gardening, in fact, appears to have been the sphere in which Chinese love of nature has especially sought to unfold itself; that perception of beauty of coloring and of nicety of detail, very general among them, shows itself here in perfection; they have long been great florists, and have delighted in writing verses upon particular flowers and fruit-trees. Garden and song were thus closely connected by them; and if one may judge from brief views received through others, their poetry has very frequently indeed something of a horticultural character. Their busy, practical habits and close inspection of detail would easily incline them in this direction; but as yet nothing grand or very elevated has been given to us by translators.

The Hebrew poets stand alone. Their position is absolutely different from that of all profane writers, and places them at a distance from the usual limits of a mere literary comparison. They only, as priests and prophets of the One Living God, beheld the natural world in the holy light of truth. Small as was the space the children of Israel filled among the nations of the earth, the humblest individual of their tribes knew that the God of Abraham was the Lord God of Hosts, and that all things visible were but the works of his hands. "The Lord made the heavens, and the earth, and the sea, and all that in them is;" they bowed the knee to no one object "in the heaven above, or in the earth beneath, or in the water under the earth." Truth is, of its nature, sublime. No fiction of the human imagination, even in the highest and richest forms which it is capable of assuming, can approach to that majesty which is her inherent prerogative. The views

UA

of the earth, open to the children of Israel, had naturally, therefore, a grandeur far beyond what the Greeks, with all the luxuriance of their florid mythology, could attain to. Of this fact—thanks to the translations of the Sacred Writings in the hands of all who speak the English tongue—any one of us is capable of judging; the extreme excellence of the Psalms, merely in the sense of literary compositions, and independently of the far higher claims they have upon mankind, has never failed to impress itself deeply on all minds open to such perceptions. The nineteenth Psalm, with the unequaled grandeur of its opening verses; the twenty-third, with its pastoral sweetness; the hundred and fourth, with the fullness of its natural pictures; the hundred and seventh; the ninety-sixth; the hundred and forty-fifth; the hundred and forty-eighth, with others of a similar character, will recur to every reader. It is generally admitted that, throughout the range of ancient profane writing, nothing has yet been brought to light which can equal these, or other great passages of the Psalms, of the Pentateuch, the Prophets, or the Book of Job. Even for sweetness, also, the old Hebrew writers were very remarkable. The most celebrated author and literary artist of modern Germany, and one little likely to have been influenced on such a subject by warmth of religious feeling, has left it as his written opinion that the Book of Ruth, usually attributed to the prophet Samuel, is "the loveliest specimen of epic and idyl poetry which we possess."[2] But the history of Jacob and his family, and the personal story of David in all its details, with other episodes easily pointed out, are almost equally full of this beautiful pastoral spirit. The same inspired pens which have dwelt on the grandest events of which time has any knowledge, have not disdained to move the lesser chords of human sympathies and affections. It was the most honored of the Prophets who so nobly recorded the greatest of all physical facts, the creation of light: "And God said, Let there be light, and there was light." And on the page immediately following, while still occupied in recording the grand successive stages of the creation, he condescends to note that out of the earth "the Lord God made to grow *every tree that is pleasant to the sight*." This simple phrase, taken in connection with all its sublime relations of time and place, has a gracious tenderness, a compassionate beneficence of detail which moves the heart deeply; all the delight which the trees of the wood have afforded to men, independently of their uses; the many peaceful homes they have overshadowed; the many eyes they have gladdened; all the festal joys of the race in which their branches have waved, seem to crowd the mind in one grateful picture, and force from our lips the familiar invocation, "O all ye green things upon earth, bless ye the Lord; praise him, and magnify him forever."

The most ancient writings of the world thus afford evidence that in those remote ages the perception of natural beauty was not wanting in the human heart. Different races and individual men may have varied greatly in giving expression to the feeling. David and Homer, the Indian and the Roman, may have sung in very different tones, but wherever intellectual life was at all active, there some strain, at least, from the great Hymn was heard.

But very early, in what may be called Christian literature, this feeling began to receive a fresh impulse and a new direction. On the same soil, and among the same races, where, in the height of heathen civilization it had never received adequate expression, both in Italy and in Greece, the eye of the believer was gradually opening to clearer and more worthy views of the creation.

"Look upward," says St. Chrysostom, "to the vault of heaven, and around thee on the open fields in which herds graze by the water-side; who does not despise all the creations of art, when, in the stillness of his spirit, he watches with admiration the rising of the sun, as it pours its golden light over the face of the earth; when, resting on the thick grass beside the murmuring spring, or beneath the somber shade of a thick and leafy tree, the eye rests on the far-receding and hazy distance."

Similar passages may also be gathered from the letters of St. Basil and St. Gregory,[3] fathers of the Greek Church. And still earlier instances of this Christian view of the earth are quoted from the writings

of a Roman lawyer, Minucius Felix, who lived in the beginning of the
third century; his evening rambles on the shores of the Mediterranean,
in the neighborhood of Ostia, were very feelingly described in pages
which have been preserved to our own time. The Christian Church
possessed a most rich inheritance in the Hebrew literature; and the
constant use of the Psalms of the Temple in her public services would
alone suffice to produce in the minds of the people a deep impression of the goodness and majesty of the Divine Creator as revealed in
his works. The Canticle of the Three Children, composed before the
foundation of Rome, and which from the early ages of Christianity to
the present hour has formed a portion of public worship, is an exalted
offering of praise with which we are all familiar: "O all ye works of
the Lord, bless ye the Lord, praise him and magnify him forever!"
And in the sublime anthem of the Te Deum we have another earnest,
unceasing expression of a feeling inseparable from Christianity: "We
praise thee, O God, we acknowledge thee to be the Lord. Heaven *and
earth* are full of the majesty of thy glory!" It is, indeed, revealed truth
only which has opened to the human mind views of the creation at all
worthy of its dignity. It is from her teaching that we learn to appreciate
justly the different works of the Deity, in their distinctive characters,
to allot to each its own definite position. There is no confusion in her
views. She shows us the earth, and the creatures which people it, in a
clear light. She tells us positively that all things are but the works of
His holy hands—the visible expression of an Almighty wisdom, and
power, and love; and as she speaks, the idle phantoms of the human
imagination, the puerile deities of the heathen world, the wretched
fallacies of presumptuous philosophy vanish and flee away from the
face of the earth, like the mists and shadows of night at the approach of
the light of day. Not one of the thousand banners of idolatry, whether
unfurled on the mountain-tops, or waving in the groves, or floating
on the streams, but falls before her. She points out to man his own
position, and that of all about him; he is lord of the earth and of all its
creatures. The herb of the field, the trees of the wood, the fowls of the

air, the fishes of the sea—every living thing that moveth upon earth—all have been given into his hand—all are subject to his dominion—all are the gifts of Jehovah.

But, ere time had enabled Christian civilization and its ennobling lessons to make any positive progress, or to produce any lasting impression on the character of general literature, the Empire was overwhelmed by races wholly barbarous. A period of darkness and disorder ensued, during which the very art of writing seems to have been all but forgotten. A few rude, unfinished sketches were all that could be expected from such an age, and in these man himself would naturally engross the attention. In societies only half civilized, man, as an individual, must always fill a bolder and more prominent position than in those where order, and knowledge, and truth are more widely diffused; he has in such a state of things far greater power for evil over his fellows; every step becomes of immediate importance, for it is associated with a thousand perils; every turn of private passion, unchecked by vital vigor of law or religion, may work out a fatal tragedy, and consequently the individual, either as tyrant, or victim, or champion, excites unceasing fear and flattery, or pity and commiseration, or gratitude and admiration. Wild legends, now warlike, now religious in spirit, naturally belonged to those centuries. No doubt the birds of heaven sang, and the flowers of the field bloomed in those ages; but we have scanty record of their existence; the eye of man was fixed on darker objects; his ear was filled with fiercer sounds.

Slowly, however, civilization and social order—those natural accessories of the Christian faith—were making progress; but the most striking efforts of reviving intelligence at this period did not assume the shape of letters. That latent poetical spirit, never wholly extinct in the human heart, sought for development during those ages through other channels. Under the hand of the religious architect, pious, though lamentably superstitious, the dignity of the forest was once more embodied in novel and imposing labors of art; scarce a fine effect of the branching woods which was not successfully repeated with

great richness of detail in Gothic stone. The beauty of the vegetation, in its noblest forms, must have been deeply impressed on the
hearts of the men who, with Teutonic patience, raised those magnificent piles. Every American familiar with the beautiful and varied effects of old forests of blended growth, where fir and pine cross their
evergreen branches amid the lighter tracery of deciduous trees, may
have often noted some single fir, rising tall and spire-like far above the
lesser grove, into the light of sun and star; some similar evergreen,
rooted in the soil of Europe, was doubtless the original of that most
beautiful of Christian architectural forms, the church spire of the Middle Ages:

> * * * * "Preacher to the wise,
> Less'ning from earth her spiral honors rise,
> Till, as a spear-point rear'd, the topmost spray,
> Points to the Eden of eternal day."[4]

It was about the time when those mediæval churches were rising
from the towns of central Europe—slow in their stately growth as the
forest whence their forms were drawn—that Troubadour and Trou-
vère, Minstrel and Minnesinger, began their wanderings in the same
region; and amid the strange medley of human passion and religious
superstition to which they gave utterance, some strains of great natural sweetness were heard. It was then that the returning cuckoo was
greeted in England with song:

> "Sumer is ycumen in,
> Lhude sing cuccu!"

It was then that merle and mavis, nightingale and lark, were saluted
with responsive music by the listening poet; it was then that daisy and
lily, *la douce Marguerite* and the *Flower of Light*, were so fondly cher-
ished and so highly honored; it was then that the May-pole was raised
in the castle court and on the village green, and that high and low, like
Arcite, hurried a-field on May-day morning "for to fetch some grene."

It was then, in short, that the blossoms and the fowls of Europe were first sung in the modern dialects of the people.

Those old wandering minstrels, troubadour and minnesinger, were, in fact, the heralds of reviving letters; they struck the first sparks of national, indigenous literary feeling in its modern forms. It was from them that Petrarch and Dante learned to speak the language of the living, rather than that of the dead. It was from their example that those great poets took, what was then a very daring step, and, rejecting the Latin, chose their native language as a medium of compositions of the highest order. How they succeeded, the whole world knows; and among the writings of those great Italian masters there are very beautiful descriptive passages, a few of which, in the form of translations, may be found in the later pages of this volume.

Fortunately for all who speak the English tongue, Chaucer, "the morning star" of British verse, as he has been hailed by Denham, followed in the track of the Italian poets; the fountains of his inspiration flowed fresh and full from his native soil. How keenly alive was he to every detail of natural beauty in the green fields of England; to the sweetness and freshness of the opening daisy; of the growing grass; of the unfolding leaf, with its "glad, light green!" He was followed by others with the same happy instincts, and a love of nature was thus infused into the earliest literature of our language. All the great poets of the sixteenth, and those of the best years of the seventeenth centuries, were more or less under the influence of this spirit— Shakspeare, Jonson, Spenser, Drayton, the Fletchers, Milton, Cowley, Denham, Dryden, Walker, Herbert, Herrick. How long is the noble roll of names of that period, who have all contributed something to our wealth in this way! There came a moment, however, when a colder and more artificial style acquired in England the same influence which long proved so paralyzing in France, when poets were content to copy those who had preceded them; when they trod the London pavement and the coffee-house floors much more frequently than the narrow paths about the fields. Mr. Wordsworth has remarked, that during a period of sixty years, between the publication of "Paradise Lost" and that of the "Seasons," all the poetry of England, with the exception of a passage or two, does not contain "a single new image of external nature." Poets were courtiers in those times, or they aimed at becoming so; they prided themselves upon a neatly turned compliment, upon a far-fetched dedication; they were wits—they were pretty fellows about town; like Horace Walpole's lively old friend, Madame du Deffand, they could very conscientiously avow, "*Je n'aime pas les plaisirs innocents!*"

Mr. Wordsworth dates the dawn of the modern era in poetry from the appearance of the "Seasons," which were first published in the year 1726. A single great work will no doubt often produce surprisingly general effects in the literary world, when the atmosphere is prepared for it. And such was the case when Thomson wrote. Many different influences were gradually combining to work out the same result. A high degree of general education, in connection with the prevalence of Christian religious truth, must always naturally dispose the mind to a more just appreciation of the works of the Deity, as compared with the works of man. The wider our views of each, the higher will be our admiration of the first. We say general civilization, however; for where the advantages of education are confined to a small class, that class will usually be found only in the large towns of a country, and its tastes and habits will therefore necessarily be more or less artificial. The rustic population, in such a state of things, will be rude, coarse, and deemed only fit for ridicule and burlesque. The poet of such a period has no sooner tried his strength, than he is eager to turn his back on the fields; he hurries "to town," to the center of all enlightenment, and soon becomes metamorphosed into a cockney or a courtier. In their day Paris and London have probably thus swallowed up many a man of genius, country born and country bred, who, had he remained in his native haunts, could never have failed in real honest feeling for that natural beauty which, like the mercy of God, is new every morning. Had Cowper lived all his days in Bond Street he

never could have written the "Task." Conceive a man like Crabbe, or
Burns, transported for life to Grub Street, and imagine what would be
the inevitable effects of the change on a spirit like theirs. But a general
diffusion of civilization produces an entirely different state of things.
An intellectual man may now live most of his days in the country without disgrace and without annoyance. He may read and he may write
there with pleasure and with impunity. A wide horizon for observation
opens about him to-day in the fields, as elsewhere. Science, commerce,
painting, sculpture, horticulture—all the higher arts, in fact—are so
many noble laborers hourly toiling for his benefit, as well as for that
of the townsman. General education is also daily enlarging the public
audience, and thus giving more healthful play to diversity of tastes.
No single literary class is likely, in such a state of things, to usurp un-
due authority over others—to impose academical fetters on even the
humblest of its cotemporaries. Whatever is really natural and really
worthy, may therefore hope in the end for a share of success. But we
conceive that it would still be possible for all these circumstances to
unite in favoring the literature of the age, without leading it into those
views of the natural world which have so decidedly marked its course
in our own day, without producing at least results so striking, a change
so marked. It is, we believe, the union of Christianity with this general diffusion of a high degree of civilization which has led us to a more
deeply felt appreciation of the works of the creation. It has always been
from lands blessed with the light of revealed truth that the choir of
praise has risen with the greatest fullness. And it would be easy, also, to
prove that those individual writers who have sung the natural beauty
of the earth with the greatest fervor of feeling and truth of description
have been more or less actuated by a religious spirit. Take as examples
the poets of our own language; how many of those who have touched
upon similar subjects were moved by what may be called Christian im-
pulses? Go back as far even as Chaucer and Dunbar, Shakspeare and
Spenser, Milton and Fletcher; if these were not all what is called religious men, yet the writings of even Chaucer and Shakspeare, though

tainted with the grossness of their times, were the works of believing
Christian hearts. If we look nearer to our own day, from the period of
Thomson and Dyer to the present hour, the fact is self-evident, and
needs no repetition of names. There have been instances, no doubt,
among the greater English poets of the last fifty years, where success
in natural description has been combined with an avowed or implied
religious skepticism. But no man can be born and bred in a Christian
community, taught in its schools, governed by its laws, educated by its
literature, without unconsciously, and, as it were, in spite of himself,
imbibing many influences of the prevailing faith. Even the greatest
English poets of the skeptical school are forced to resort to what appears to the reader a combination of an imperfect, enfeebled Christianity with an incomplete and lifeless Paganism. Their views of the
material world almost invariably assume a Greek aspect; and we must
adhere to the opinion, that, in spite of their florid character, their grace
of outline, their richness of detail, these fall unspeakably, immeasur-
ably short of the grandeur, the healthful purity, the living beauty, the
power and tenderness of feeling which belong to revealed truth. With
the Greek, as with so many others, man was, more or less palpably,
the great center of all. No so with the Christian; while Revelation al-
lots to him a position elevated and ennobling, she also reads him the
lowliest lessons. No system connects man by more close and endear-
ing ties, with the earth and all it holds, than Christianity, which leaves
nothing to chance, nothing to that most gloomy and most impossible
of chimeras, fate, but refers all to Providence, to the omniscient wisdom of a God who is love; but at the same time she warns him that
he is himself but the steward and priest of the Almighty Father, responsible for the use of every gift; she plainly proclaims the fact, that
even here on earth, within his own domains, his position is subordinate. The highest relation of every created object is that which connects it with its Maker: "For thy pleasure they are, and were created!"
This sublime truth Christianity proclaims to us, and there is breadth
enough in this single point to make up much of the wide difference

very true

between the Christian and the heathen poet. And which of these two views is the most ennobling, each of us may easily decide for himself. Look at the simple flower of the field; behold it blooming at the gracious call of the Almighty, beaming with the light of heavenly mercy, fragrant with the holy blessing, and say if it be not thus more noble to the eye of reason, dearer to the heart, than when fancy dyed its petals with the blood of a fabled Adonis or Hyacinthus? Go out and climb the highest of all the Alps, or stand beside the trackless, ever-moving sea or look over the broad, unpeopled prairie, and tell us whence it is that the human spirit is so deeply moved by the spectacle which is there unfolded to its view. Go out at night—stand uncovered beneath the star-lit heavens, and acknowledge the meaning of the silence which has closed your lips. Is it not an overpowering, heartfelt, individual humility, blended with an instinctive adoration or acknowledgment in every faculty of the holy majesty of the One Living God, in whom we live, and move, and have our being? And where, at such a moment, are all the gods with which Homer peopled his narrow world? An additional sense of humiliation for the race to which we belong, and which could so long endure fallacies so puerile, weighs on the spirit at the question, and with a greater than Homer we exclaim: "O worship the Lord in the beauty of holiness; let all the earth stand in awe of Him!"

A distinguished living poet of England, Mr. Keble, has a very pleasing theory in connection with this subject. In his view, the three great divisions of poetry belong naturally to three successive periods of the world: the epic flows from the heroic youth of a race; the drama, with its varied scenes and rival interests, from the ambitious maturity of middle age; while, as civilization advances farther in the cycle of time, the human heart oppressed with the strife of passion, the eye wearied with the restless pageant of vanity, turn instinctively to more simple and more healthful sources of enjoyment, and seeking refreshment from the sweetness and beauty of the natural world, give expression to the feeling in the poetry of rural life. In this sense the verse of the fields—the rural hymn—becomes the last form of song, instead of being the first. Something similar to this has doubtless often been the course of individual life; many of the greatest minds and best hearts of our race have successively gone through these different stages—the aspiring dream of youthful enthusiasm, the struggle in the crowded arena of life, and the placid calm of thoughtful repose and voluntary retirement under the shade of the vine and the fig-tree. Happy will it be for the civilized world, for these latter ages of the earth, if such should indeed prove the general course of the race! Most happy will it be for us, the latest born of the nations, we who belong to the aged times of the world, if such should be our own direction!

Probably there never was a people needing more than ourselves all the refreshments, all the solace, to be derived from country life in its better forms. The period at which we have arrived is rife with high excitement; the fever of commercial speculations, the agitation of political passions, the mental exertion required by the rapid progress of science, by the ever-recurring controversies of philosophy, and, above all, that spirit of personal ambition and emulation so wearing upon the individual, and yet so very common in America, all unite to produce a combination of circumstances rendering it very desirable that we should turn, as frequently as possible, into paths of a more quiet and peaceful character. We need repose of mind. We need the shade of the trees and the play of healthful breezes to refresh our heated brow. We need the cup of water, pure from the spring, to cool our parched lips; we need the flowers, to soothe without flattery; the birds, to cheer without excitement; we need the view of the green turf, to teach us the humility of the grave; and we need the view of the open heavens, to tell us where all human hopes should center.

Happily, in spite of the eagerness with which our people throw themselves upon every rallying point of excitement, they are by no means wanting in feeling for a country life. It is true they delight in building up towns; but still, a large portion of those who have a choice look forward to some future day when a country roof shall cover their heads. They hurry to the cities to grow rich; but very many take pleasure in returning at a later hour to their native village, or at least put up a suburban cottage, with a garden and grass-plat of their own. The rural aspect which has been given to our villages and smaller country towns, and which is often preserved with some pains—the space between the buildings, the trees lining the streets and shading every wall, with the little door-yard of flowers—all these are evidences of healthful instincts. But another, and very striking proof of the existence of the love of nature in our people may be found in the character of American verse. A very large proportion of the poetical writing of the country partakes this spirit; how many noble passages, how many pleasing lines, will immediately recur to the mind as the remark suggests itself; scarce a poet of note among us who has not contributed largely to our national riches in this way; and one often meets, in some village paper or inferior magazine, with very pleasing verses of this kind, from pens quite unknown. Probably if an experienced critic were called upon to point out some general characteristic of American poetry, more marked than any other, he would, without hesitation, declare it to be a deeply-felt appreciation of the beauty of the natural world.

But although as a people we have given ample evidence of an instinctive love of nature, yet we have only made a beginning in these pleasant paths. There still remains much for us to do. This natural taste, like all others, is capable of much healthful cultivation; it would be easy to name many steps by which, both as individuals and as communities, it lies in our power to advance the national progress in this course; but to do so would carry us beyond the limits allotted to our present task. It is hoped, however, that we may be forgiven for detaining the reader a moment longer, while we allude at least to one view of the subject which is not altogether without importance. The social condition of Christendom has, in many respects, very materially changed within the last fifty years. Town and country no longer fill what for ages seemed the unalterable relative position of each. A countryman is no longer inevitably a boor, nor a townsman necessarily a cockney; all have, in their turn, trod the pavement and the green turf. This is especially the case in America; the life, the movement in which our people delight, is constantly bringing all classes into contact, one with another, and diffusing the same influences throughout the entire population. Something of that individuality which gives interest and variety to the face of society is lost in this way; but, on the other hand, we gain many facilities for general improvement by these means. The interchange between town and country has become rapid, ceaseless, regular, as the returns of dawn and dusk. But yet, in spite of the unbroken communication, the perpetual intermingling, there still remains to each a distinctive, inalienable character; the moving spirit of the town must always continue artificial, while that of the country is, by a happy necessity, more natural. We believe that the moment has come when American civilization may assume, in this respect, a new aspect. The wonderful increase of commercial and manufacturing luxury, which is characteristic of the age, must inevitably produce a degree of excess in the cities; all the follies of idle ostentation and extravagant expenditure will, as a matter of course, flourish in such an atmosphere, until, as they expand right and left, they overshadow many things of healthier growth, and give a false glare of coloring to the whole society which fosters them. There are many reasons why our own towns are especially in danger from this state of things; they have no Past; they lack Experience; Time for them has no individual teachings beyond those of yesterday; there are no grave monuments of former generations standing in the solemn silence of a thousand warning years along their streets.

Probably there never has been a social condition in which the present is more absolutely absorbing, more encroaching, in fact, than in our American towns. The same influences may extend into the country; but it is impossible for them to be equally powerful in the open fields, where they are weakened by the want of concentration, and by many counter-acting circumstances. The situation of the countryman is in this sense favorable; he is surrounded by great natural teachers, by noble monitors, in the works of the Deity; many are the salutary lessons to be learned on the mountain-tops, within the old groves beside the flowing stream. The everlasting hills—the ancient woods—these are his monuments—these tell him of the past, and not a seed drops from his hand but prophesies of the future. The influences which surround the countryman are essentially ennobling, elevating, civilizing, in fact. Strange as the remark might have appeared a hundred years ago, we shall venture deliberately to repeat it at the present hour: We conceive the spirit which pervades country life to-day, to be more truly civilizing in its nature than that which glitters in our towns. All that is really desirable of the facilities of life may now be readily procured in the fields, while the excesses of luxury and frivolous fashion are more easily avoided there. Many different elements are blended in the composition of true elegance, and some of these are of a very homely, substantial nature; plain common sense, and even a vein of sterner wisdom are requisite; that moderation which avoids excess is absolutely indispensable; order and harmony of combination are needed; dignity and self-respect are essentials; natural feeling must be there, with all its graceful shades of deference and consideration for the rights and tastes of others; intellectual strength, which has no sympathy with the merely vapid and frivolous, is a matter of course; and while cheerfulness and gayety, easy and unforced as the summer breezes, should not fail, yet a spirit of repose is equally desirable; it is evident, also, that a healthful moral tone is requisite, since, where this is wanting, the semblance of it is invariably assumed; and to all these must be added that high finish of culture which years and reflection can alone give. What element is there among these which may not be readily fostered in country life? On the other hand, that very concentration which was formerly so favorable to the progress of the towns, is now producing injurious effects by leading to excesses, and perversion of healthful tastes. The horizon of the townsman becomes fictitiously narrowed; he needs a wider field for observation—greater space for movement—more leisure for reflection. He learns to attach too much importance by far to the trappings of life; he has forgotten, in short, the old adage: "*Non è l'abito che fà il monaco!*" It can scarcely, therefore, be an error of judgment to believe that while in past generations the country has received all its wisdom from the town, the moment has come when in American society many of the higher influences of civilization may rather be sought in the fields, when we may learn there many valuable lessons of life, and particularly all the happy lessons of simplicity.

AUTHOR'S NOTES

1. Unwilling, for a moment, to be supposed entitled to credit to which she can lay no just claim, the writer of these remarks hastens to avow that whatever opinions she may have formed on subjects connected with ancient literature, have been entirely drawn from translations. Although it is impossible to enjoy the full perfection of a great poem in any other than the original language, yet we are enabled, by means of the best versions, to form general views regarding a work, and to appreciate, at least, the spirit with which it is imbued.

2. Goethe.

3. These translations have all been transcribed from M. de Humboldt's pages.

4. Camöens.

Preface to the 1868 edition
of *Rural Hours*

EIGHTEEN years have passed since the first publication of these Rural Notes. Each of these eighteen years has brought clouds and sunshine of its own to the valley, where these Notes were written, and to its homes.

There have been changes that are striking—changes that were very painful—during these years; and yet, beyond all doubt, each event has been wisely and graciously ordered for the best. The Lord gave, the Lord hath taken away, blessed be the name of the Lord.

The little town itself is somewhat altered. Eighteen years cannot pass over an American village, even when remote from the great thoroughfares of traffic, even when quite beyond the whirl of speculation, without bringing somewhat of growth, somewhat of progress. Nay, we are now beginning to assume certain airs of importance to which the rustic borough of 1850 could lay no claim. The telegraph wires run through our streets. It was St. Jerome, I believe, who asserted as a striking fact that, thanks to the pilgrims and palmers of his time, a good Christian in Britain might hope to hear tidings of a brother in Egypt, within the course of four or five months. A message sent at Easter might confidently be expected to be delivered by Michaelmas. The stage-coach bearing the mail moved at a palmer's pace, eighteen years ago. But to-day, like other good Yankees, we expect to hear what passes at London the day before it occurs. Moreover, we read the telegrams by gas-light. And—must we confess the degradation?—a railroad is approaching, stealing gradually along the banks of the Susquehanna, until it is expected to reach the lake shore with next winter's snow!

One scarcely knows whether to mourn or to rejoice over this event in our history. Progress, alas, is not always improvement. We were rather proud of our seclusion. We were not in the least anxious to hear the whistle of the locomotive so close at hand. We even flattered ourselves that our position was impregnable, that steam could never climb our hills. But the engineers have won the day—*nous avons changé tout cela*—and since Alps and Andes have been compelled to submit to the iron yoke, the Alleghanies must needs bow the neck also. With as good a grace as possible, we must endeavor to console ourselves by boasting of the conveniences of modern civilization, and talk of breakfasting at home, and dining in New York—a journey which our fathers made somewhat after the pilgrim fashion, thinking themselves fortunate if, with fair wind and weather, they accomplished it in ten days.

And even if the shrill whistle of the black afrite of speculation be heard in the valley, we need not, for all that, make worldlings of ourselves. We may be countryfolk still. We may be as rustic as we please. The hills, and the woods, and the lake, may still afford us true delight. The valley and the forests have never looked more lovely, more luxuriant, than during these charming June days. The birds are singing as sweetly, the flowers are blooming as gayly, as freshly, as they did eighteen summers ago.

Later Hours

May 25th, 1868.—Early this morning there was great agitation in the tree-tops waving near us. For an hour, or more, there was high tragedy hovering over the pines and maples. The birds, of course, are in the midst of their spring joys, and family cares, and they are very numerous this year, more so than usual. The large pine overshadowing our cottage roof, at the northward, has several nests, and appears a favorite resort of the robins. Early in the morning a great hawk came sailing over the river, from the eastern hills, and wheeling in airy circles above the pine. Indescribable agitation fell upon the robins; their anxious, hurried flight about their nests, coming and going, wheeling and watching, was painful to see; their cries of horror, of wrath, of indignation, as the tyrannical hawk drew nearer and nearer, and at last, alighted on the pine, were truly distressing. Oh, for a gun! Oh, for a sportsman's hand and sportsman's eye, to aim straight at the heart of this Gessler of the woods! But alas, the female garrison could do nothing beyond playing the part of the sympathizing chorus in the Greek tragedy, while Niobe was mourning over her slaughtered children. In a moment, perhaps fifty robins, and other small birds, had gathered about the pine, utterly fearless for themselves, but full of sympathy for the afflicted households of their brethren, and mad with powerless rage against the hawk. Oh, for a valiant king-bird to put the monster to flight, by boldly dashing at his eyes, as king-birds often do! But alas there was neither man, nor king-bird, near enough to avert the catastrophe. With the utmost coolness the hawk perched himself near a nest, and after helping himself to a young robin, utterly regardless of the turmoil and agony around him, sailed proudly away. Per-

[handwritten marginal note: Kill the hawk to protect the robins? Isn't that harm of God?]

haps some fifteen minutes passed, and again the wicked wretch came
sailing over the meadows, towards the pine. The same agitation, or
rather increasing agony, among the robins followed—they appeared
absolutely frantic with anxiety for their brood, and wrath against the
invader. But, of course, it was fruitless. The arrogance and impudence
of the hawk were intolerable to behold. He picked out another nestling
from the young brood, and again sailed away. Four or five times during the course of an hour he repeated the same performance, sailing
grandly over the river, alighting on the pine, picking out a young bird
first from one nest, then from another, and on each occasion flying
away with the utmost composure, though a score of light skirmishers
were fluttering in impotent rage, about him. Alas, for the bereaved
mother-birds, and their mates—their sharp cries of grief were heard
throughout the day—the agitation among the whole feathered tribe
in our neighborhood continued more or less until evening.

May 27th.—Reading in Mr. Knapp's "Journal of a Naturalist," I
observe that he mentions the word *wilt* as a provincialism, in some
parts of England. This verb is very generally used in America, and de-
serves a word of defence more than most terms of the kind. It would
seem to have a meaning of its own scarcely expressed by any other
synonym; it signifies neither to "wither," to "blight," to "die," or to
"decay." If we understand the word rightly it means something of de-
bility, and drooping, akin to faintness in animal life, but implying ca-
pability of restoration. There is thus a shade of distinction in the word,
which at times may approach to poetical delicacy, and which redeems
it from a place with others of the same class.

To "hawl," or "haul" is also placed among the provincialisms of
his neighborhood by Mr. Knapp; but this is assuredly a good English
word. Johnson gives it, with a derivation from the French "haler" to
draw. With Johnson for our authority, we need not give up this old
verb.

May 28th.—The hawk has again made his appearance, attacking a
nest on the opposite side of the house, to the great anguish of the bird-

people in that direction. We have noticed the first bereaved pair of robins almost hourly since the cruel onslaught upon their nest—they are generally fluttering close to the house, or perched on some branch where we see and hear them—the sharp cry of trouble and sorrow is peculiar, and cannot be mistaken.

May 29th.—The poor little robins are consoling themselves; they are building a new nest, and they have chosen a very singular position. They have determined to be safe from the wicked hawk this time—and they have come to us for protection. We had noticed them fluttering about near the house quite frequently, with a sort of look of melancholy observation. This morning one was observed with a straw in its mouth flying towards the front door—and now, this evening, the beginning of a nest is plainly seen directly over the front door of the house, almost within reach. It is a spot sheltered indeed from the hawk. Even his sharp eyes cannot see it, for it is protected by the roof of the veranda. They have chosen a canny spot—between the antlers of a deer, which are nailed above the front door!

Some fifty years ago, there was an association of sportsmen in this county, called the "Unadilla Hunt." They met at stated times during the sporting season, and hunted the last bears, and panthers, and deer found in Otsego county. Some five and thirty years since, these gentlemen very kindly sent the author of the "Deerslayer" half a dozen antlers from the very last deer shot by the "Hunt." The gift was received with great pleasure. One of the antlers was nailed up over the front door of Otsego Hall within the house, another in the entrance tower without. They remained there until sad changes came, and the house passed into the hands of strangers. Soon after, it was destroyed by fire, and when a little cottage was built with the bricks and oaken wood-work of the dear old homestead, then in ruins, over the same oaken doors, in their new position, were placed the antlers which had been nailed there under circumstances so different. It is between these antlers, that the poor little persecuted robins have taken shelter. We have many fears, however, that the nest, though fairly begun, may never be finished. There is so much opening and shutting of the front door, so much passing to and fro, that they may leave their task unfinished. If one could make them understand how safe they are—how little they have to fear—how very much we are their friends, all would go well. But who can talk robin to them!

May 30th.—A severe gust this evening—the wind unusually high for about five minutes—the trees in great agitation, waving grandly in the blast. The pines in the church-yard have suffered—several large limbs have been broken—and the ground is strewn with smaller twigs. As we were sitting quietly in the parlor, suddenly a loud noise was heard, a crash, and then a fall—we ran to the window, and with amazement discovered that one of the blinds had been forcibly lifted from its hinges by the gust, and thrown against the railing of the veranda. A most singular freak of the wind—actually raising a heavy blind perpendicularly from its hinges. After the shower was over, we went out and examined the blind—it was uninjured—not a slat broken—the hinges in perfect condition. Before the shower this blind was, like the others, in its usual position, flat against the wall of the house, but it could not have been secured, as the others were. The hinges were of a peculiar kind, a socket covering a pivot—very simple in construction. We hear that a barn-door in the village was blown from its hinges by the same gust—but in this last instance the hinges were broken.

Our robins have not been driven away by the clatter of the storm. Their nest has quite a finished look, and they have been seen perched on the antlers this evening—possibly congratulating themselves upon being under cover.

June 1st.—The flowers, though later than usual, owing to the cold April, are coming out in great profusion.

We have now two new additions to our Flora on the lake shore. Water lilies, the beautiful white lilies, now bloom freely in several of the shallow bays. Some few years since, there were none of these lilies in Lake Otsego, though abundant in some of the streams of the neighborhood. It is said, that fifty years ago they were found here, but they were plucked too freely, and died out. Such is the tradition. Quite recently they have been planted in two or three of the bays, and are now increasing rapidly.

The second addition to our botanical treasures has produced quite an excitement in the village—among the ladies at least, and all who love flowers. A few years since, it was a well-established fact, that no laurel was known to grow upon our lake shores—none had ever been seen in the many walks of those who were accustomed to explore the hills and woods of the neighborhood. No laurel had been seen—no laurel had been heard of. But, two summers since, as a party of ladies were walking on the eastern hills, over ground often visited before, in past years, they suddenly came upon a clump of the true white laurel! It seemed as if they must have grown up at that spot by enchantment. Great was the triumph of the discoverers—great was the surprise in the village, and great the delight of the lovers of wild flowers. Possibly the birds may have brought the seed here, and the young plants may have been passed unnoticed, till of a size to flower. Laurel abounds some forty miles further south, near Unadilla.

June 3d.—The robins are actually in full possession of their nest. They have shown great good sense, and wonderful persistence since they began to build—there has been much more movement on the veranda than usual—the lattice work near them has been brushed and cleaned—the vines have been tied up—and the painters have also been at work above and below them. There has been some one in sight almost every hour of the day—working among the flower-beds, or on the veranda—while men, women, and children have been passing to and fro. Poor little creatures—some needless alarms they must have had—but doubtless they wisely decided that we meant them no real harm. I never yet saw a nest in a position so trusting, so confiding— and having known their previous troubles, we feel doubly interested

in them. One is reminded of the lines of George Herbert, who, one
summer's day, dissatisfied with the little good he believed himself to
be doing, wished himself a tree, for the sake of sheltering the birds:

> I read and sighe, and wish
>   I were a tree,
> For sure then I should grow
> To fruit, or shade; at least,
> Some bird would trust
> Her household to me,
> And I should be just.

I hope that we shall be just to the poor little robins, and guard them
from all dangers so far as we can.

June 10*th.*—Pleasant drive with our friends, down the valley. Saw,
for the first time, the earliest approaches of the railroad. Far away,
in a quiet meadow on the opposite side of the valley, a newly-built
"shanty" of boards rose conspicuous in contrast on the greensward—
and a little further on the highway, we passed another close at hand,
a mere shed of yellow boards. They are going to turn the course of
the river, by opening a new channel, at one point, thus avoiding the
building of two bridges. The Susquehanna is a very winding stream,
throughout its long course—the Indian name is said to signify, the
winding river. It was impossible to look at those rude, yellow shanties,
built on the summer grass, amid the buttercups and daisies, without
some of the grave thoughts which belong to all harbingers of the future—they foretell a new era to this quiet valley. May the iron rails
bring far more of good, than of evil, to the headwaters of the Susquehanna!

June 15*th.*—Of all the wonders performed by that modern magician, steam, there is not one, perhaps, which could have been so little
foreseen, so little foretold, as its possible effects upon bird history.
Birds have always been great travellers. From the first years of the

Creation, with the changing seasons, they must have moved northward or southward. Such is the usual course of their immigrations.
Never, perhaps, have they made long, regular annual journeys, eastward or westward. Occasionally, a wanderer from one continent,
driven by the winds, alights in some very distant region, where his
tribe is unknown, like the Passenger Pigeon, said to have been found
in England. But, as a general rule, the birds of the eastern and western
hemispheres are quite distinct in their species, until you reach the region of the extreme north, where the resident birds are frequently the
same on both continents. This might be expected. But the Mocking-
bird, the Humming-bird, the Oriole, nay, even the hardy and strong-
winged Passenger Pigeon, have all been for ages peculiar to America,
just as the European Red-breast, the Lark, and the Nightingale are
peculiar to Europe.

But a change seems now at hand, and this change has been effected
by steam. Some of the more pleasing birds of Europe have been carried
in steam vessels from England to Australia and to New Zealand, where
they are becoming domesticated. And we have all heard of the European sparrows now becoming the public pets of New York, on account
of their usefulness in clearing the trees from insects. Both the Lark
and the Nightingale have also been introduced successfully, it is said,
though in small numbers, into parts of our Atlantic coast. How strange
it will be, if those two famous birds should ever raise their charming
strains from our fields and groves, in company with the Bob-link and
the Wood-thrush!

[margin note: hand of God, introducing birds to new continents]

The voices of those two noblest of the singing-birds of the old world
would indeed form a charming addition to our native choir. There is
something peculiarly delightful and spirited in the song of the Lark.
"It is," says W. Mudie, "more joyous in the sun, more inspirable by the
life which the solar influence diffuses through the atmosphere, than
almost any other creature: not a spring air can sport, not a breeze of
morn can play, not an exhalation of freshness from opening bud, or

softening clod can ascend, without note of it being taken and pro-
claimed by this all-sufficient index of the progress of nature. She rises
not like most birds, which climb the air upon one slope, by a succession of leaps, as if a heavy body were raised by a succession of efforts, or with pauses between; it towers upward like a vapor borne
lightly in the atmosphere, and yielding to the motion of the air, as
vapors do. Its course is a spiral gradually enlarging. The accordance
of the song with the mode of ascent and descent is also worthy of
note. It gives a swelling song as it ascends, and a sinking one as it
comes down; and even if it take but one wheel, as the wheel always
includes ascent and descent, it varies the pitch of the song. Every one
in the least conversant with the structure of birds, must be aware that
with these, the organs of intonation and modulation are *inward*, de-
riving little assistance from the tongue, and none or next to none,
from the mandibles of the bill. The windpipe is the musical organ,
and it is often very curiously formed. Birds require that organ less for
breathing than any other animals, because of the air-cells and breathing tubes with which all parts of their bodies—even their bones—
are furnished. But these different breathing organs must act with less
freedom when the bird is making the greatest efforts in motion, that
is, when ascending or descending, and in proportion as these cease to
act, the trachea is more required for the purpose of breathing. The skylark thus converts the atmosphere into a musical instrument of many
stops, and so produces an exceedingly wild, and varied song—a song
which is perhaps not equal in power, or compass, in the single stave,
to that of many warblers, but one which is more varied in the whole
succession."

The lark is entirely a bird of the free and open country—the downs,
and pastures, and meadows of Europe. The nightingale, on the contrary, is often heard during the months of May and June, in the gardens
of cities, during the early morning and the late evening hours. There is
a discussion as to the character of the nightingale's song, some writers
calling it cheerful, others plaintive. The celebrated English statesman

Charles Fox was very critical on this point; here is a letter of his on the subject. He considered their song cheerful:

"Dear Grey,

In defence of my opinion about the nightingales, I find Chaucer—who of all poets seems to have been the fondest of the singing of birds—calls it a *merry note*. Though Theocritus mentions nightingales six or seven times, he never mentions their note as plaintive or melancholy. It is true, he does not call it anywhere *merry*, as Chaucer does, but his mentioning it with the song of the blackbird, and as answering it, seems to imply that it was a cheerful note. Sophocles is against us; but he says, "*lamenting Itys*," and the comparison of her to Electra is rather as to perseverance, day and night, than as to sorrow. At all events, a tragic poet is not half as good authority on this question, as Theocritus, and Chaucer. I cannot light upon the passage in the "Odyssey," where Penelope's restlessness is compared to the nightingale's, but I am sure it is only as to restlessness that he makes the comparison. If you will read the last twelve books of the "Odyssey," you will certainly find it, and I am sure you will be paid for your hunt, whether you find it or not. The passage in Chaucer, is in the "Flower and the Leaf." The one I particularly allude to in Theocritus, is in his "Epigrams"—I think in the fourth. Dryden has transferred the word *merry* to the goldfinch, in the "Flower and Leaf"—in deference, may be, to the vulgar error. But pray read his description of the nightingale there; it is quite delightful. I am afraid I like these researches better than attending the House of Commons.

Yours affectionately,
C. J. Fox."

Here are the passages referred to by Mr. Fox: The first is from Chaucer's "Flower and Leaf."

> The nightingale with so *merry a note*
> Answered him, that all the wood rong

> So sodoinly, that as it were a sote,
> I stood astonied, so was I with the song
> Thorow ravished, that till late and long
> I ne wist in what place I was, ne where:
> And agen, me thought, she song ever by mine ere.

Dryden's version follows:

> A goldfinch there I saw, with gaudy pride
> Of painted plumes, that hopp'd from side to side,
> Still perching, as she paus'd; and still she drew
> The sweets from every flower, and suck'd the dew;
> Suffic'd at length, she warbled in her throat,
> And tuned her voice to many *a merry note*,
> But indistinct, and neither sweet, nor clear.
> Her short performance was no sooner tried,
> When she, I thought, the nightingale replied:
> So sweet, so shrill, so variously she sung,
> That the grove echoed, and the valleys rung;
> And I so ravish'd with her heavenly note,
> I stood entranc'd, and had no room for thought;
> But all o'erpower'd with an ecstasy of bliss,
> Was in a pleasing dream of Paradise.

The passage from the Odyssey is given below:

> As when the months are clad in flowery green
> *Sad Philomel*, in bowery shades unseen,
> To vernal airs attunes her varied strains
> And Itylus sounds warbling o'er the plains;
> Young Itylus, his parents' darling joy,
> Whom chance misled the mother to destroy,
> Now doom'd a wakeful bird to wail the beauteous boy.
> *So in nocturnal solitude forlorn*
> A sad variety of woes I mourn.

Introduced birds (handwritten annotation)

The voices of the lark and the nightingale may be heard in echoing accompaniment, throughout the prolonged choir of European poets, from the early dawn of civilization to the present hour. There are few poems of any length, in either of the languages of Europe, in which some allusion to one or the other has not a place. The noblest poets of the earth were born companions to these birds; beneath skies saluted by the lark, among groves haunted by the nightingale. These little creatures sung with Homer and Sappho among the isles of Greece, for Virgil and Horace on the plains of Italy; they cheered Dante in his life-long wandering exile, and Petrarch in his solitary hermitage. Conceive the joy with which Chaucer, Shakspeare, and Spenser listened, each in his day, among the daisied fields of England, to music untaught, instinctive, like their own! What pure delight, indeed, have these birds not given to the heart of genius during thousands of springs and summers! How many generations have they not charmed with their undying melodies! They would almost seem by their sweetness to have soothed the inexorable powers of Life and Death. Were an old Greek, or an ancient Roman to rise from the dust this summer's day—were he to awaken after ages of sleep, to walk his native soil again, scarce an object on which his eye fell would wear a familiar aspect, scarce a sound would strike his ear, but would vibrate there most strangely. Yet, with the dawn, rising from the plain of Marathon or the Latin Hills, he would hear the same noble lark which sung in his boyhood; and with the moon, among the ilexes and olives shading the fallen temple, would appear the same sweet nightingale which entranced his youth.

June 23d.—Charming drive to Middlefield. Never was there a more lovely June than the present month—lawns, gardens, meadows, forest, all so richly luxuriant, so bright and flowery, so fragrant and so fresh.

The bee tribe are said to be more numerous than usual. The flowers are full of them. In passing a farm-house we saw one of the pollarded young maple saplings before the door blackened with a large swarm of honey bees. A few of the little creatures flew about the carriage as we passed, but without alighting.

"A bee among the flowers in spring is one of the cheerfullest things that can be looked upon. Its life appears to be all enjoyment; so busy, and so pleased." Any one who has wandered about the fields during the summer months will assuredly agree with this opinion of Paley. The very hum of the bee, as it flies past us on its pleasant errand, in quest of some sweet flower, or returning with its dainty load, is one of the most cheery of the voices of summer. The movement of the little creature, also, is full of meaning, and attracts the eye, as curiously characteristic of its nature; it generally flies in lines more or less direct; we see here nothing of the idle roaming, vagrant flight of the gaudy butterfly, and nothing of the hesitating, doubtful, over-cautious pause of the plodding ant. The instincts of the bee are all lively and vigorous; it seems conscious that wherever grass grows, there some blossom will be found to reward its search, and it moves steadily onward until a head of clover, or perchance some prouder flower, offers the precious drop. And, alighting to gather its grateful harvest, how skilfully its work is carried on; other insects may show as much cleverness in attaining their end, but there are few, indeed, which accomplish their task so pleasantly. The wise little bee does no mischief; no violence marks her labors; the freshness of the flower remains unsullied by her passage; she leaves the gay petals and the green foliage alike uninjured. No plant suffers for her visits! There is nothing unsightly, nothing repelling or painful in any of her measures; all is order, nicety, and harmony.

June 24th.—Evening drive to the Point. Country and lake lovely, as they must always be under a soft summer sunset. But the clouds were our especial delight. Noble masses brilliantly white rose to a great height just above Mt. Vision, seeming to rest on the forest, now luxuriantly green. Elsewhere the heavens were clear, and deeply blue. Gradually the silvery white of the clouds, so inexpressibly beautiful, so pure, so spiritual in character, changed to hues more brilliant, ev-

ery shade of rose and crimson passing in turn over that Alpine world
of vapor. It was wonderful to see all those evening glories hanging
over the eastern hills! The coloring of the western sky was bright, but
far less vivid. One might have believed this the hour of dawn, rather
than the close of the day. Frequently the same effect of high and brilliant coloring may be observed at sunset, through every degree of the
eastern horizon, from north to south—and at times when the coloring westward, is much more sober. I am too ignorant to account for
this. I have even fancied that this sort of mirage, was more frequent in
our valley than elsewhere—but the impression is probably produced
by greater frequency of observation. This evening, those noble fields
of vapor, unearthly in their beauty, and imposing in their magnitude
and elevation, continued varying in brilliant coloring for more than
an hour—while elsewhere the heavens, were blue, or pearly with twilight grey.

There is no earthly object with which the human eye is familiar, so
full of grandeur, of majesty, and at the same time of tender beauty, and
delicate sweetness, as the clouds which float over our heads.

"O ye Clouds bless ye the Lord, praise Him, and magnify Him, for
ever!"

June 26th.—The robins have successfully raised their little family; four eggs were laid, the mother-bird sat patiently brooding over
them, one large dark eye occasionally turned downward, as we stood
watching; at times some needless alarm would drive her from her nest
for a moment—but all has gone well with the young brood nevertheless. In due time four ugly little heads appeared, four voracious
yellow bills were opened—and now, all have taken flight; Robin and
Pecksey, and Flapsey and Dicksey are gone! Among all the robins
fluttering about the grounds, we cannot tell which are our own, but
we may yet discover some partiality for the veranda which may point
them out.

The empty nest, as it rests on the antlers, is to remain where the
good robins built it, as long as Time shall spare it.

June 28th.—They are building a new school-house, the first, worthy of the purpose, that this village has ever seen. It will be of bricks, ample in size, and with all modern improvements. One looks on with anxious hopes, desiring that it may indeed forward the education of our children, in the right direction.

American education—how much should that term imply! With all the facilities at command which the utmost freedom of action, united to means the most ample can give—with all the wisdom of past ages, all the experience of older nations open to us—how much should we accomplish!

As yet we have done but little. We are still not much beyond our A, B, C. We still depend too much upon the spelling-book. We still give too large a place to book-learning. According to our present scheme the knowledge that comes from books, and by that means, the sharpening of the intellect for practical purposes, these are the chief elements of common American education. But a nation may boast, very justly, of a general diffusion of instruction, may be even very far advanced in science, very skilful in adapting scientific knowledge to practical purposes, and yet be, at best, a half-educated people. Instruction is but a part of education. True education must be harmonious, must be complete, must cover the whole ground. It must keep in view the great ends of human existence. It must train the individual in the healthful development of every higher power and faculty, and it must teach him to devote all those powers and faculties to worthy purposes. True education must influence alike body, mind, heart, and soul. Its teachings are not partial, but general. Its whole action is healthful. It has no exaggerations. It has no false aims. It is never overstrained. It is thorough in every lesson. It is conscientious in every step. It is wise in all its purposes. It goes to the heart of things. It throws to the winds all small ambitions. It knows how to value humble virtues; simple attainments have their place in its teachings. Its one great aim is how best to fit the individual for leading a worthy life; how best to prepare him for the position he is likely to fill; to qualify him, in short, for serving *himself*, *his neighbor*, and *his Creator*, according to the best of his ability.

Such an education includes many elements too often overlooked by common American theories. Temperance in the pursuit and in the enjoyments of wealth, moderation in our ambitions, the incalculable value of such quiet virtues as Contentment, Cheerfulness, and Peace, the high dignity of perfect Truth, of perfect Integrity, of true Humility, of a just Subordination,—these are too often forgotten. The great importance of plain common sense, of a true perception of the fitness of things, of simplicity, of good manners, of good taste, which is merely the flower of that sturdy plant good sense—all these and other similar points receive much less attention than they deserve.

Material prosperity, and not the worthy discharge of plain duties, is too often held up as the great object to be striven for with ceaseless, restless effort, and exhausting toil. Truth, Peace, and Happiness are too often sacrificed in this way.

The country which produced a Washington—one of the very noblest models of manhood the world has yet seen—should assuredly know how to place aims the most worthy before its children. But this subject of American education is one much too great to be properly considered in half an hour, of a warm summer's day.

July 2d.—Shall the new railroad move northward, from this point, along the lake shore, or shall it take the more easy, and more natural course, following the adjoining valley of the Oaks, to meet the Utica route at Richfield? And at what point in the village shall the station be built? These are questions of all-absorbing interest to our good people just now. Many of us are very desirous that the lake shore should not be broken up, and our beautiful woods devoured by the fiery breath of the iron horse. Wood, not only for fuel, but for lumber, and other useful purposes, is every day becoming more valuable. If the railroad destroys our forests it will greatly lower the market value of every farm it has shorn in this way. It will render the hills and valleys colder in winter, and dryer in summer. And if the track passes along the bays, and makes stagnant water, it will bring here, as it has done elsewhere, intermittent fevers, and chills and fever, thus far almost unknown here. No; let the iron horse feed upon coal, and not wood—and let the track follow its natural course through the valley of the Oaks, avoiding wherever it goes, the making of stagnant pools.

July 4th.—A very warm day, and a very quiet one. The thermometer 90° in the shade. No movement in the village, beyond a few family gatherings in the gardens, to gratify the children with fireworks.

The most impressive Fourth of July we have ever known in this village was that of 1865, when, with deeply grateful hearts, we kept our Thanksgiving for the return of peace, after those fearful years of strife and struggle.

The beat of the first drum which called our men to arms, can never be forgotten by any who heard it. The stroke seemed to fall upon our very hearts. The thought that brother was arming against brother was appalling. Never had the probability of such a struggle occurred to our people in this part of the country. They were taken by surprise. They were astounded. They paused, for a while, in dismay—in natural horror. And then came the stern awakening. Every hamlet and valley in the county sent out its brave young men; from the farms, the workshops, the commercial houses, and the professional offices, side by side they marched to uphold the Flag of the Union, the emblem of constitutional government, law, and order. Had they failed in that noble defence, anarchy and violence, under every hideous form, must have been our lot. That they were acting on the defensive—that the first blow was not from their hands, that no other course was possible to honorable men, became the greatest consolation, the best ground for hope, to the women who, with grave and anxious grief, saw them marching away.

And after those years of fierce strife—those years of agony—how great was our joy, when, on that soft summer's day, the Fourth of July, 1865, we held our Thanksgiving for the happy close of the terrific

struggle—for the blessed return of peace! A hundred flags were floating over the village homes; cheerily rung the church-bells; while the
salutes from the cannon echoed and reëchoed finely from the mountain sides.

In the evening, under the moonlight, the town was gayly illumi-
nated, with far greater brilliancy, far greater unity of design, than was
ever known here before; and over the door-ways, in letters of light,
was inscribed the blessed word, PEACE!

Village Improvement Societies

AMONG the substantives in common use, which have very materially changed their meaning within the last two centuries, we may include the word village. This is a common noun which represents, to-day, an entirely different combination of ideas from those which it conveyed to the minds of our ancestors two hundred years ago. The English village, in the reign of the Stuarts, could boast little of the character of "Merry England" in its outer aspect. Hedges and orchards, a little green, and a May-pole were there, perhaps,—not always, however,— and a lowly church, old and ivy-covered, such as George Herbert worshipped in, may have appeared in the distance. But these were the pleasing touches in a picture where the foreground was entirely filled up by gloomy and rudely built cottages, too often—as a general rule, indeed—mere hovels, scarcely better than the sheds for cattle. Low, dark, and coarsely put together, with earthen or stone floors, and a bit of casement scarcely large enough to let in the sunlight which the good God gives to all, those dwellings must have looked very little like the homes of free-born Christian men. We know, indeed, and thanks to God that it is so, that actual human affection and simple piety have often carried a glow and a blessing into dwellings as dark as those. But as a general rule, the outer aspect of things, and the inner life of the English village of that period, must have been very cheerless. The sole inhabitants of those low-thatched cottages were persons of the lowest grade. Only a generation earlier, some of them had been serfs, attached to the glebe. There were serfs in England as late as the reign of Queen Elizabeth of glorious memory. The heavy clouds of ignorance and superstition which covered Europe so densely in the Mid-

64

[handwritten top margin: Shitty Villages in the 1600's]

dle Ages, had not yet entirely rolled away, and these shadows were nowhere darker, or heavier, than over the villages. There were, no doubt, brave and manly hearts, and sweet womanly faces coming and going through those humble cottage door-ways, but all active and intelligent spirits invariably crowded into the towns and larger cities. Village life was considered utterly hopeless; it was entirely given up to stagnant ignorance, poverty, and stupidity. Penury and discomfort were the common lot. Even within doors, the few pieces of household furniture of the good wife, the rude bed, the heavy table and settle, and the utensils for cooking, were not many degrees better than the pottery, the bark, and wickerware, and the calabash of the Indian women of Virginia and Massachusetts. Scarce a ray of the civilization of the great cities, of the Castles and Halls of England, penetrated to her villages. In the days of Shakspeare, and Bacon, and Spenser, your Hobbinol and Lobbinol, and Diggory, your Mopsa and Dorcas, were all dull and loutish, scarcely knowing B from bullsfoot. All the difference of centuries lay between the burgher of the city and the boor of the village.

[handwritten right margin: Contrast to the other reading]

And the French villages of the same date were no better. When our Huguenot ancestors fled through Normandy and Gascony, driven to the sea-board at the point of the sabre, before the *dragonnades* of the great Louis and his Jesuit confessors, what was the character of the villages through which they passed? What was the country village of France all the time when Versailles was in its glory? The houses themselves were perhaps somewhat more substantial in strength of material and workmanship than those of England, but they were equally gloomy, dark, comfortless, and even more filthy. The donkey, the cow, the pig, and the poultry often shared the dwelling with the peasant and his children. The natural gayety of the French character drove the people from such gloomy dwellings abroad into the open air for all their hours of relief. Their recreations were exclusively of a public character; the dance, the merry-making, the village *fête* were all kept up in the open air. And so were their occupations. Even the women and children toiled in the fields. Like the cattle, the peasants and their families were seldom in the cabin, unless at night. The people were naturally industrious, frugal, quick-witted and cheerful. But the sombre villages into which they crowded for safety were gloomy, squalid, and filthy in the extreme. Jacques Bonhomme, the peasant of France, was weighed down by ages of oppression and superstition. In the time of Madame de Sévigné, the good curé of a village in Brittany received from Paris a handsome present of a clock. The news spread through the parish, and the people came crowding to see the wonder. So great was their amazement on beholding the movement of the works, and hearing the sound of the hammer striking the hour, that they fell on their knees and said an Ave. "*C'est le bon Dieu!*" they exclaimed. It was with difficulty the good curé could raise them from their knees. After all, from worshipping the image of a saint to worshipping a clock is but a step—and that not altogether an irrational one. Madame de Sévigné, clear-headed and warm-hearted as she was, only laughed at the story. It should rather have made her weep. But what were the wretched peasants, in their village hovels, to the lady of the Court of the Great Louis? It may be doubted if she had ever crossed the threshold of one of the peasants of her barony of Sévigné. Even to walk through one of those squalid, gloomy, filthy villages, would probably have appeared to her impracticable. And yet she was a good, sincere, warm-hearted Christian woman. But, as in England or even more so in France, the distance between human life in the village and human life in the towns seemed immeasurable, impassable.

How different is the state of things to-day, and in our own country! Village life as it exists in America is indeed one of the happiest fruits of modern civilization. Our ancestors, familiar with the English and French villages, could never have dreamed of all the many striking differences which would appear two centuries later in the village homes of their own descendants in the New World. The idea would never have occurred to them that the remote village could ever share so freely in the enlightenment and civilization of the capital city. But

steam, the great magician, serves the rustic to-day as faithfully as he
serves the cockney. Comforts, conveniences, new inventions, striking improvements are scarcely known in New York and Philadelphia,
before they are brought to the villages, hundreds of miles in the interior. You find there every real advantage of modern life. Your house
is lighted by gas—and, if you choose, it is warmed by steam. The
morning paper, with the latest telegram from Paris or London, lies
on your dinner-table. The best new books, the latest number of the
best magazines, reach you almost as soon as they reach the Central
Park. Early vegetables from Bermuda, and early fruits from Cuba,
are offered at your door. You may telegraph, if you wish it, to St.
Petersburg, or Calcutta, by taking up your hat and walking into the
next street. This evening you may, perhaps, hear a good lecture, and
to-morrow a good concert. The choice musical instrument and the
fine engraving may be found in your cottage parlor. What more can
any reasonable being ask for, in the way of physical and intellectual
accessories of daily life? And in addition to these advantages of modern civilization shared with the cities, there are others of far higher
value, belonging more especially to country life. The blessings of pure
air and pure water are luxuries, far superior to all the wines of Delmonico, and all the diamonds of Ball & Black. And assuredly to all eyes
but those of the blindest cockney, the groves and gardens and fields
and brooks and rivers make up a frame-work for one's every-day life
rather more pleasing than the dust-heaps, and omnibuses, and shop-
windows of Broadway. And, happily for the rustic world, the vices,
the whims and extravagances—the fashionable sin, the pet folly—of
the hour are somewhat less prevalent, somewhat less tyrannical on the
greensward than on the pavement. There is more of leisure for thought
and culture and good feeling in the country than amid the whirl of a
great city. True, healthful refinement of head and heart becomes more
easy, more natural under the open sky and amid the fresh breezes of
country life. Probably much the largest number of the most pleasant
and happiest homes in the land may be found to-day in our villages

and rural towns—homes where truth, purity, the holiest affections, the highest charities and healthful culture are united with a simplicity of life scarcely possible in our extravagant cities. And these advantages, thanks be to God, are not confined to one class. Even the poorest day-laborer in the village, if he be honest and temperate, leads a far happier and easier life than his brother in the cities. The time may come, perhaps, when the cities—greatly diminished in size—shall be chiefly abandoned to the drudgeries of business, to commerce and manufactures during the hours of day, and deserted at night; when the families of the employers and laborers shall live alike in suburban village homes. In the present state of civilization, every hamlet within a hundred miles of a large city may be considered as one of its suburbs. In former centuries, he was a wise man who left the village for the city. To-day, he is wise who goes to the city as to a market, but has a home in the country.

But while this, our nineteenth century, has given such happy development to village life—and especially so in America—there is, of course, still room for improvement. We have not yet achieved perfection. There are many finishing touches still needed. And many of these lesser improvements are simple and inexpensive in execution, while they are singularly effective in their results.

The general aspect of an American village is cheerful and pleasing. The dwellings have an air of comfort, they turn a friendly face to the street, they are neat and orderly in themselves and in their surroundings; their porches and verandas, their window-blinds without and shades within, their door-yards and their trees, are all pleasing features forming the general rule, to which the exceptions are rare. But while such is the usual state of things, still in every American village we have yet seen there is room for much improvement. And these desirable improvements are many of them simple and easily brought about, requiring only a moderate fund, placed in the hands of judicious persons—requiring, in short, a local *Society for Village Improvement.*

The work of such a society would vary, of course, with the position, character, size, and actual condition of each particular village. The more characteristic such improvements are, the more closely they are adapted to the particular individual nature of each village, the greater will be their merit. The finishing touches for a village on the prairies, or one on the sea-shore, or one in the Green Mountains, in Oregon, or in Texas, should, of course, vary very greatly in some of their details. But the spirit, the intention, must be everywhere the same. To render the village, in whose service we are working, more healthy, more cheerful, more attractive—to add to its usefulness, its respectability, its importance, its pleasantness—to increase, in short, its true civilization, that is to be our aim. To improve our villages becomes a matter of even greater importance than to improve our cities. A very large proportion of American *homes* are to be found in the villages, and in the smaller towns, which always preserve much of their original rural character. More than half the population of our largest cities have no *homes*. They crowd into hotels or boarding-houses. They are essentially Bohemians. The largest of our cities, especially New York, the greatest of all, were long ago called mere *Bivouacs*. Half the young men you shall meet to-morrow in Broadway have no homes in the great city. Their legal domicil is in New York; but their true home is still to be found in some village-cottage, where the annual holiday visit is paid to father, mother, and sister. Nay, it is so with many a married couple, who have no better home in the busy city than the boarding-house room, but who take flight, with their little ones, every summer, to the parental home, often hundreds of miles from the Battery.

Hygienic improvement should form one of the first subjects for consideration, by the Village Improvement Society. Where a village is incorporated, its Trustees should of course carry out, or forward to the utmost, every work of this kind. But village corporations, like those of the cities, are often inert. The private speculations of A, B, C, often interfere with progress of this kind. Mr. Green will not subscribe

to some particular improvement because his own property will not
manifestly increase in value by it. Mr. Brown would assist freely if the
bridge or the sidewalk were a hundred yards nearer to his own house.
A common movement, a general impulse is wanted; and this is what
our Society supplies. A permanent, voluntary society of respectable
character, composed of influential persons, acts as a general stimulant
to torpid corporations and to unmanageable individuals. By talking,
writing, speech-making, and printing, it increases the general activity,
even in cases where the corporation should be the regular agent. An
ample supply of pure water should be the very first step in our work.
Pure water is absolutely indispensable for health, for cleanliness, for
respectability—and as a protection against fire an ample supply is far
more effectual than all the salamander safes in the country. Let water,
then, be our first object. A good bath-house, under respectable man-
agement, either public or private, should be opened. All drains should
then be looked after. The proper ventilation of every public building should be brought about, if possible. All pools, or marshes, where
stagnant water can accumulate, should be filled up at the earliest day.

The streets and sidewalks, the roads, lanes, paths, the bridges and
the wharves—if such there be—should be looked after, and improved
to the utmost. Good construction and constant neatness are the points
to be especially considered. Where there is a bridge, let it be architectural and picturesque, if possible, as well as safe and durable. Give us
a stone bridge wherever you can, and plant a creeping vine or two at
the base; a Virginia creeper, a clematis, or a trumpet creeper, would
greatly improve the beauty of such a bridge, without injuring the
stonework. As regards the streets, trees in greater numbers will probably be wanting in some of them. Choose the right sorts, and plant at
proper distances—not so very near as to crowd the branches. Watch
over those already planted, and if caterpillars or injurious insects appear, remove them at once. Of course, your streets should be protected
by confining all cattle, pigs, poultry, to the grounds of their owners.
Fierce war, a war to extermination, must be waged against *all weeds*

found growing in the streets, by the road-sides, in door-yards, or in waste places. This is a step which will do more for the neatness of the village, for the good of its gardens, than perhaps any other you could name. Our farmers and country-people in general would seem to have a peculiar weakness for weeds. But it is a miserable economy which shrinks from giving half a day to uproot, or cut down, weeds which next summer may injure a whole crop. The number of noxious weeds allowed to grow in some of the best streets of our most beautiful villages is truly surprising.

Perhaps the neatest arrangement for village sidewalks, excepting in the business streets, is that already found in some parts of the country—a narrow strip of pavement, bricks or flags, with a wide border of neatly-cut grass each side of it, and a double row of trees overhanging the walk. The plank sidewalks must soon disappear, as timber becomes so very valuable. And a sidewalk entirely paved—without the border of grass on each side—is too much opposed to all rural ideas.

And here we would have a word to say on the naming of our village streets. There is work for the Improvement Society in this direction. A Main street there must always be in every village, and as the word expresses the idea, the name is appropriate and natural. But why, pray, should every hamlet have its Broadway? Main street is clearly in much better taste. The names of trees are always pleasing in village streets; maple, elm, chestnut, birch, oak, pine, tamarac, locust, cedar, catalpa, sycamore, and others, have a pleasant sound, and are appropriate wherever such trees are found, either as the natural growth, or in cultivation. The great Quaker, William Penn, seems to have been the first builder of cities who turned to the trees for the names of his streets. The idea may therefore be called American, adapted to the whole country. And these form a class of names of which one never wearies. It is singular that while William Penn made this poetical choice for half his streets, for the other half, cutting them at right angles, his notions were all dry and mathematical; he was the first, I believe, to number the streets from *one* to *one hundred*. This numbering the streets

is not much to the fancy of many of us. There may be some excuse
for this course in a large city growing so rapidly that people have no
time to pause and think on the subject. But in a village, the practice
becomes absurd and inexcusable. After naming some of our streets
from the trees, let us remember the birds who build their nests in them.
It must be a luckless village indeed which cannot find scores of nests
in its streets, to say nothing of its gardens and neighboring groves.
Robin, wren, swallow, sparrow, martin, chicadee, thrush, pewee, or
phœbe, oriole, the eagle, the hawk, the heron, the woodpecker, the
quail, the grouse—these and others of the same kind would be appropriate wherever such birds are found. In the same way, the names of
the wild animals, once tenants of the ground, would have the merit of
variety, and natural association, with a sort of historic interest. Beaver,
bear, stag, elk, deer, moose, would be appropriate for almost any new
village. The natural features of the ground, such as lake, river, cliff,
rock, brook, hill, spring, offer another class of names. The artificial
works suggest others; such as wharf, bank, school, church. And the
names of the older families who occupied the site of the village in its
earliest days, have an interest of another kind. All these would surely
be preferable to numbers one, two, three, or even to Broadway, Pall-
Mall, and the Boulevards.

From the streets we turn to the door-yards. Every member of our
Village Improvement Society should stand pledged to keep his, or her,
door-yard in the neatest possible condition. First banish every weed.
Next keep the grass closely cut, and then plant a few pretty shrubs
and flowers, as many as you can without overcrowding the space, always leaving grass enough for a contrast, a framework for your flower
pictures.

In walking through every village—sometimes at the very heart of
the little town—we shall find here and there spots capable of great improvement, at very little cost—some point where a tree or two, with
a bench beneath their shade, would form a pleasant resting-place for
the weary; at some turn in a road, or a street, or where two roads

meet—at some point which offers a pleasing view, on the outskirts of the village—beside a spring, beneath a bank, near a picturesque rock, on the bank of a brook, near a bridge—there is not a village in the country where several such spots might not be pointed out, capable of great improvement in this way. A few trees planted in a group—not in a row—unless in an avenue—with a bench beneath, and creepers climbing over the trunks and branches of the trees, would form an inviting seat for many a weary creature. In Switzerland, and in some parts of Germany, such benches in the shade are quite common; occasionally, they stand near a cross, or some modest monument on which a line or two from some poet, or a verse from Holy Scripture, has been engraved.

Every village should, of course, have its Green, or playground, or common, or playstow, or pleasaunce—any thing but a park, unless you can show your fifteen or fifty acres—where old and young, the grave and the gay, lads and lasses, fathers, mothers, and children may meet together on a summer's evening to breathe the fresh air, and chat with their neighbors. Such a ground need not be large. Even one acre well laid out, and in a good situation, with groups of trees and shrubbery, with winding walks and benches for rest, may be capable of giving great pleasure to the townsfolk. But, of course, four or five acres would afford much more variety. If possible, let there be a neat fountain, or some simple local monument in the centre, to add to the interest; a monument to some worthy public character of the neighborhood, or a stone recording some local event of general interest.

One of the pleasantest public walks known to the writer may be found in a village of Southern Germany. A little stream, in fact a mere brook, flows near the village. Following the bank of this brook, in all its windings, a broad walk has been made, with a border of turf on either side, varied with groups of trees and clumps of shrubbery, and patches of flowers, and pleasant rustic seats, the whole being included within a narrow strip of ground perhaps fifteen yards in width. On one side lie the open, unfenced fields, on the other is the flowing brook.

Along this pleasant path one may wander for more than a mile, enjoying much variety in the simple rustic views opening on either side. The cost of this charming walk must have been trifling, since the amount of land, fit for cultivation, given up to it, can be scarcely more than a few feet in breadth, the useless bank of the brook being included within the fifteen yards devoted to it. It is kept in beautiful condition at very little expense. The people of those old countries in Europe are so highly civilized in these respects, that they never injure a tree, or a shrub, or a branch in their public walks. They have too much good sense and good manners for such misdemeanors.

Many Americans are now at Dresden, a city very rich in its public walks and gardens. One of these walks is so peculiar, that we mention it as a happy instance of the way in which even the oldest towns in Europe, more especially on the Continent, have laid out pleasure-grounds within their city limits. The walk to which we allude is simply an old street, running through part of the town, but now turned throughout its entire length into a garden. It is built up with good houses on either side, each house having its ample door-yard filled with shrubs and flowers. Between these door-yards—where one would naturally expect to find a paved street—there is, in fact, a garden. There is a broad gravel walk in the centre, and gravel sidewalks immediately in front of the houses; while trees, and shrubs, and grass, and flowers give to the whole the character of a garden. At the crossings, where other streets cross it at right angles, there are light bars and turnstiles. When it is necessary that a cart or a carriage should enter, the bar is removed. But the houses have access to other parallel streets in the rear, for business purposes. This garden-street is a very pleasing feature of Dresden, and might assuredly be imitated in our American towns.

Wherever spacious church-yards do not exist, there our Village Improvement Society should suggest a quiet, well-kept cemetery, in a retired and pleasing situation, well shaded with trees and shrubbery and divided by neat walks. Every hamlet and rural neighborhood should indeed unite to form such a resting-place for their dead. Those sad and solitary and desolate family grave-yards, often choked with weeds, seen on our farms, are unworthy of our present civilization, and the very last to be adapted to a state of society in which land is constantly changing hands.

The protection of the birds becomes another duty for the local Improvement Society. The birds naturally form a happy element in all village life. Very many varieties prefer the neighborhood of man; they gather about the village homes from choice. Even in the open country, as you drive along the highways, you frequently see half a dozen nests in the orchard, or in shade trees near a farmhouse, while the trees, at a greater distance, are apparently untenanted. Many nests are seen in the streets of every village, but where the laws are most faithfully carried out, there the summer concert will be the richest, and the sweetest, and the fullest, there all weary eyes will be most frequently cheered by the sight of those happy little creatures; there your gardens will be most free from noxious insects, there robin, there blue-bird, and song-sparrow, and pewee, and goldfinch, and oriole, and cat-bird, and wren, shall carol their thanks to you from March to November.

The machinery for carrying out the work of a Village Improvement Society is by no means difficult to manage. Let a well-written, well-digested plan be printed. After a few prominent persons are sufficiently interested—men and women of good sense, good taste, good feeling—then call a public meeting. Offer your plan for adoption, settle your Constitution and By-Laws, elect your officers, and go to work as soon as possible. The broader the basis of your constituency, the greater will your success be, since the larger the number of hands and heads interested, the more will be the work you accomplish. But it is probable that at the outset there will be, in many villages, great indifference, possibly some positive opposition. Do not heed this. Your object is good, praiseworthy, desirable; move onward, therefore, and begin your work, though it be on a small scale. If you work prudently, before five years are over, the indifference and the opposition will be

sensibly weakened; when ten years have passed, the ground will be
yours. The whole village will work with you. The good results will
be manifest to even the poor blind. Where it is thus necessary to begin with few members, give your attention first to your own door-
yard and streets—improve them in every way you can; set out trees,
plant shrubs, destroy the weeds, put up bird-houses. Go to the Trustees of your village, and get their permission to work on some one of
those points capable of improvement, to which allusion has already
been made. Choose, for instance, a grassy spot, where two or three
streets meet; set out three or four good-sized trees in a group, place a
bench beneath them, destroy the weeds, and keep the turf in good condition. Public attention will soon be attracted, and, in the end, public
favor must necessarily follow. Every year would increase the number of members and the amount of the fund. It is well in such cases
that subscriptions should vary from twenty-five cents to twenty-five
dollars annually. The children should be interested, as a means of education. And even the very poor and ignorant should be invited to
become members, out of good fellowship, and as a step in general civilization. Only persevere, and you will succeed. Perseverance alone
often brings about temporary success, where the object is unworthy.
But wherever the object is really deserving and the fruits of a work
are good, there perseverance is one of the most effective allies you
can desire.

Two or three annual lectures on some subject connected with the
work of the Society would be very desirable. Flowers, gardening,
shrubbery, trees, the husbandry of woods and groves, fountains, road-
making, bridges, sidewalks, pavements, would form subjects, with a
hundred others of a similar character. Several public meetings in the
course of the year would also be pleasant, meetings where short papers
and letters connected with the work of the Society would be read, and
short conversational speeches made.

A public ground for summer pic-nics should also be provided, within a short distance from the village—purchased, planted, and im-

proved by the Society, and a general village gathering held there every year, during the pleasant weather.

Whatever calls the attention of our people from mere money-making, or small politics, whatever provides harmless recreation, subjects for pleasing thought, for healthful action—whatever, in short, contributes pleasantly to the physical, moral, and intellectual good of the people, and to a true advance in Christian civilization, must assuredly prove a real, substantial benefit to us all. — How is any of it a "substantial benefit"

Otsego Leaves I:
Birds Then and Now

ANY ONE who has had the happiness of living in a country-home, and on the same ground, during the last twenty years, must naturally have been led to observe the birds flitting about the gardens and lawns of the neighborhood. And it matters little whether that country-home be in a village or among open farms. Many birds are partial to a village-life. The gardens and fruit-trees are an attraction to them. Nay, there are some of the bird-folk who seem really to enjoy the neighborhood of man. Among these are the wrens, the robins, the cat-birds, and, to a certain extent, the humming-birds. These lovely little creatures no doubt enjoy the Eden of the flower-garden, rather than the neighborhood of Adam and Eve. They have no objection to the human race, however they endure our presence. And there can be no doubt that any ten acres of village-gardens will show you many more humming-birds during the midsummer hours between early dawn and the latest glimpse of twilight than can be found in the same extent of wood or meadow. These little creatures take especial delight in flitting about the flower-gardens in the evening, at the very moment when family groups gather on the verandas, and will often fly within arm's-length. They seem proudly conscious that their marvelous flight—rapid, is it not, beyond that of any other earthly creature?—will carry them half the length of the garden before that clumsy being, man, can rise to his feet. Who ever caught a humming-bird in flight? A humming-bird on the wing you may perhaps have captured; more than half their lives would seem to be passed on those quivering wings. They feed on the wing always. Of all the feathered tribe few so well deserve the

epithet of birds of the air. Seldom do you see one at rest. While pois-
ing itself before some honey-yielding flower with that inconceivably
rapid quivering of the wings, the humming-bird may occasionally be
caught, but the achievement is not a common one. In actual flight it
may be doubted if one ever was caught. Confident in their marvelous
power of wing, they linger lovingly about the flower-garden while
human forms are very near, and human voices are chatting in varied
tones, and no doubt clearly heard by them. Few birds, excepting those
belonging to the night, are out so late. They must have a large acquaintance among the fire-flies, the katydids, the gay moths, and the hooting
owls. Doubtless the fragrance of the flowers, always more powerful in
the dewy evening hours, proves the attraction. They do not, however,
always visit the sweetest blossoms, they seldom poise before a rose or
a lily, but they know very well that roses and lilies do not live alone;
gathering about those queenly flowers, they will be sure to find a brilliant company yielding the sweets they seek. Whatever may be the
cause, they are arrant little rovers, in the latest twilight and in the early
moonlight. There are, indeed, few hours in the twenty-four when that
silent sprite, the humming-bird, may not be found darting to and fro
around our village homes.

   That delightful singer, the merry house-wren, so delicate in form,
so cheery in his ways, so lively, so fearless, so sweet and joyous in his
song, is a fast friend of mankind, seeking from preference to build near
us. It is a social little creature, often building within range of eye and
hand, and almost cheating one into the fancy that his sole object is to
sing for the amusement of his neighbors. He will begin a delightful
strain close to a window, perched on a flowering shrub perchance, or
swinging to and fro on a waving spray of some creeping vine, and
sing half an hour away with little interruption. No one can hear one
of his joyous bursts of song without being convinced that the wren
sings with pure pleasure, out of the fullness of his happy little heart.
The birds sing to us nothing but Truth. In this sense, their songs are
pure as hymns. There is no leaven of evil in their music. And they

clearly delight in their gift of song. It is said that, on some happy occasion, when Jenny Lind had been surpassing herself at a charity concert,
she exclaimed, joyously, "Es ist doch schön dass ich so singen kann!"
("Is it not charming that I can sing so!"). And if we understood the
language of the wren, we might perhaps discover the same feeling of
happy wonder at his own performance. His summer life seems to be
more than half song. He will sing in the warmest noontide hours, when
other birds are silent. He will sing on cloudy days, when other birds
are moping. But perhaps his choicest, most gleesome, most musical
melody, is sung after a shower, from the head of some tall weed, and
beneath the rainbow. He sings for the pleasure of his wife. He sings for
the instruction and entertainment of his numerous little family. Sometimes one sees him flying toward his nest with a very eager, busy look,
as if occupied with some affair of vast importance; in another moment
he is out again, perched on the same twig where you have often seen
him singing as if music were his only object in life. Nevertheless, he
is anything but an idle creature, a regular busybody in fact, a great
builder of nests, a very kind husband, and an excellent father to his
comical little children, who cluster together full of fun and play, but
rather helpless, and who are watched by their parents and fed by them
long after they have left the nest. And, happily for us, through all his
family cares he sings away merrily and sweetly beneath our windows,
ever generous with his music.

As for the robins, every one knows that portly, honest, sensible-
looking creature, the first bird to return to the village in the early
spring-days, and the last to leave us. They are often very tame. And
no wonder: many of them were doubtless born on some window-sill,
or under the eaves of your own house, perhaps. We once had a very
friendly acquaintance with a robin family, which lasted during three
years. The parent-birds, frightened from their first nest in a pine-tree
on the bank of the Susquehanna by a cruel and rapacious hawk, who
devoured their first brood under the very eyes of the poor father and
mother, took refuge in very close neighborhood to us, beneath the

roof of a veranda over the front-door of a cottage-home. There they seemed to feel perfectly safe, and took little heed of the coming and going of the family. They lingered very late that first year, the different members of their family flitting about the house, frequently on the roof of the veranda, or on the window-sills. The following spring, to our great pleasure, they returned, and, no little to our surprise, repaired the old nest over the front-door, and raised another family in it. They seemed to become even more tame, were not disturbed by the painters at work on the veranda, and continued to hover about the house more or less during the whole summer. The autumn was mild, and they lingered very late. At last there were light falls of snow, and the nights grew cold. At this moment a young robin, full-grown, but one of the summer brood, was observed to be often perching on a lower limb of a tree shading the veranda in summer-time, but now bare, of course. He would sit there by the hour, with his head turned toward the house. Early in the morning, on first opening the blinds, there was robin on his favorite limb. Late in the November twilight, there sat our robin, generally looking into our windows, as it were. Food was thrown on the roof of the veranda, but he ate little of it. All through November, until the last leaves had fallen, we saw our little friend more or less frequently. At length, he seemed to be the only robin left about the place, but there he was, looking toward the house when we opened the blinds at daylight. There he was still seen after the first snow-storm, when the gray limb where he perched was covered with snow. We watched him now with affectionate anxiety, and wondered at his perseverance; the last red berries of the mountain-ash had been eaten, the red haws of the thorn had all been harvested, and yet he sat there for an hour or two every day. It was not until the 11th of December that we missed him, after a cold, stormy night.

The next spring, the third season, there was a nest under the veranda, but not over the door; we fancied they were young birds, perchance our young friend of last December, though of this we could not of course be sure.

The cat-birds—what a wretched name, by-the-by, for a fine singer!—though not so numerous as the robins, often build in our villages, and are sociable and friendly. Those you meet in the woods are
shy, and flit away among the flickering shadows as you draw near. Not
so those whose parent-nest was placed in some garden-shrub. In the
village which is the writer's home, there was some years since a luxuriant, old-fashioned flower-garden belonging to a venerable couple
who took pleasure in working themselves, among the flowers, even in
their old age, and both lived beyond fourscore. This garden became a
favorite haunt of the cat-birds and the humming-birds for many years.
Whether the flowers were an attraction we cannot say—the gay coloring may have pleased them, but probably the number of insects, their
lawful game, was the inducement to build year after year on the same
ground. In this garden was a pleasant arbor of primitive style, and near
the arbor stood a fine crab-apple-tree. Here the old gentleman and the
old lady would frequently rest awhile after working among their flowers. There had always been cat-birds about the place—that is to say
always in the American sense of the word—some fifty years, perhaps,
or since the ground had been first broken for a garden. But when the
garden became well shaded, and the crab-apple had grown to be a tree,
a pair of these birds built yearly among the apple-boughs, or in close
neighborhood to the arbor. And here they sang their choicest songs
with high glee. The old gentleman worked daily through the summer
near the arbor, and the cat-birds became very intimate with him. They
would fly about his head, perch on a twig in full sight, and hop down
to pick up a worm close to his spade or hoe. They seemed, indeed, to
take actual pleasure in his society. When they saw him coming with
hoe or rake to his usual task, they would flutter out to meet him, and
wish him good-morning in one of their odd cries, but end by singing
him a sweet song. And this intimate friendship between the old gentleman and the cat-birds continued not only through one season, from
May to October, but during several successive summers—five or six
years indeed. The writer has often seen and heard them. They would

tolerate other visitors to the arbor in company with their old friends, but if you went alone you were treated very shabbily—they became saucy, and, peering curiously at you from a safe distance, would begin to make fun of you with one of their mocking cries.

Then, twenty years ago, robins, wrens, cat-birds, and humming-birds, and, indeed, the whole summer flock, were certainly more numerous than they are to-day. Some observers believe that the number of summer birds has diminished more than half. The same species are still with us, but how long will they remain, when every year we note, perhaps, half a dozen on the same lawns where they were formerly counted by the score? *Now* you may sit on a garden-bench a long summer morning, and very possibly not see more than one oriole, one blue-bird, one greenlet, one yellow-bird. Even the robins come hopping about the garden-walks by two and three, instead of the dozen who were formerly in sight at the same moment. And the humming-birds are very perceptibly less in numbers. One has to watch for them now in the summer twilight; presently you shall see little ruby-throat hovering alone about the honeysuckles; and perhaps, half an hour later, his wife, little green-breast, may come for a sip of sweets. But that is all. Rarely, indeed, do you see four or five quivering, darting, flashing about among the blossoms at the same moment, as one often saw them in past years.

The gregarious birds, too—the purple finches, the wax-wings, the red-wings—are only seen in small parties compared to the flocks that visited us twenty years ago.

And winter tells the same story. Not that the regular winter birds are so much less numerous than they were—probably there is little change among the sober snow-birds, the merry chicadees, or the winter-sparrows. These will probably gather about our doors in January in much the same groups and small flocks that we saw here formerly. The woodpeckers and the blue-jays are less numerous, however. The crows seem to hold their own, and in mild weather come flapping out of their favorite haunts in the woods, to take a look at

the village. But winter offers a mode of guessing at the number of
the summer population, which is a pretty fair test, so far as the tree-
builders are concerned. When the leaves fall in November, the nests
are revealed, and after snow has fallen, and each nest takes a tiny white
dome, they become still more conspicuous. The Indian tribes count
their people by so many lodges or *tepées*; in the same way, during the
autumn and winter months, we may count the tree-building flock of
the previous summer by their nests. And these tree-builders are probably a fair proportion of the whole summer flock, including those who
build among the bushes or on the ground. It has often been a winter
amusement of the writer, when walking through the village-streets,
to count the birds'-nests in the different trees in sight. The trees are
all familiar friends, and the nests of different kinds add no little to
their interest. But, alas! every four or five winters one observes the
number of nests diminishing. Among the maples and elms lining the
streets, or standing on corners, or rooted on garden-lawns but overhanging the sidewalks, were certain individual trees which were apparently especial favorites; their gray limbs never failed to show year
after year several of these white-domed nests. Here among the forked
twigs of a young maple was the bold, rather coarsely-built nest of the
robin, shreds of cloth or paper, picked up in the door-yards, hanging perhaps loosely from among the twigs. Yonder, on the drooping branch of an elm, near the churchyard-gate, was seen the long,
closely-woven, pensile nest of the brilliant oriole. Here, again, not far
from the town-pump—a primitive monument of civilization dating
from the dark ages of village history, but still highly valued and much
frequented by the present generation, although the little town now
boasts its "Croton"—a maple of good size was never without a nest in
spite of the movement and noise about the pump. There were several
of these trees which showed every year two or three nests; and one,
a maple differing in no way from other maples so far as one could
see, and standing near a corner before the door of a parsonage, the
branches almost grazing the modest windows of the house, revealed

every winter three, four, or even five, and one year six, nests on different branches, from the lowest to the highest. There were often two robins' nests, with the pendulous nest of the greenlet, and one of the goldfinch, and occasionally one of a summer yellow-bird, or of a small pewee. The tree is still standing, gay with brilliant coloring, gold and red in varied shades, at the moment we are writing; but, so far as one can see, there has been but one nest on its branches during this last summer. Such was the story told by the village-trees *then*; you were never out of sight of some one nest, and frequently half a dozen could be counted in near neighborhood. To-day it may be doubted if we have more than one-third of the number of these street-nests which could be counted twenty years ago.

This is a sad change. These are the facts which would seem to account for the diminished number of the summer flock. Young boys, scarcely old enough, one would think, to carry a gun, are allowed to shoot the birds with impunity in the spring, when they are preparing to build, or even when their eggs are actually in the nest. This should not be. The law against shooting certain birds at that season should be enforced. It is now a dead letter. Then, again, look at your daughter's hat. Dead birds cannot build nests; they cannot sing for our joy and their own delight; they are mute, but, unhappily, they are considered a pretty ornament when pinned down among ribbons, flowers, fruits, beads, and bugles, on that composite exaggeration to which Fashion, forsooth, has given the name, but not the uses, of a hat. All the smaller birds, with any beauty of plumage, are now murdered to satisfy this whim of Fashion. When we remember the millions of women, young girls, and children, in the country, and bear in mind that most American women require three or four hats in a year—some of them a score or two—we can imagine how many yellow-birds, ruby-throats, greenlets, etc., are required to pile up the holocaust. One sees sometimes even girls who are half-babies wearing a humming-bird in their tiny hats. Not long since the writer saw a pretty young girl wearing impaled on one side of her hat a Mexican humming-bird, on the other

a fiery-crest kinglet, while the wing of a blue-jay stood boldly up be-
hind. One frequently sees parts of two or three different birds on the
same hat—wings, or tails, or heads. Alas! why will our young maid-
ens, pretty, and good, and kind-hearted in other matters, be so cruel
to the birds? They would scold their little brothers for stealing nests
or eggs, but they have no scruple whatever in wearing a dead bird in
their hats!

A third cause of the lessened number of some species of our summer birds may be found in the fact that so many are now eaten at the
South, by the caravan of travelers, when they are plump and in good
condition from feeding on the many seeds and berries which form
their usual winter harvest. "Small birds" are included in the bill-of-
fare of every hotel in the warmer parts of the country from November to March. This is perfectly natural, and one has not a word to say
against the dainty dish of "four-and-twenty rice-birds baked in a pie"
to set before the invalid traveler. But the great number of this class of
travelers now moving southward every winter has no doubt been one
cause of diminishing the flock of our summer birds. Travelers who in
January breakfast on robins and rice-birds in Florida cannot expect to
hear them sing the next spring in their home-meadows.

But, whatever be the cause of this marked difference of numbers
between the summer flocks *then* and *now*, that difference becomes a
grief to us. We miss our bird-companions sadly; we miss them from
their haunts about our village-homes; the ear pines for their music,
the eye longs for the sight of their beautiful forms flitting gayly to and
fro. Still more serious, however, is the practical consequence of this
wholesale slaughter of the smaller birds. The increase of insects is a
tremendous evil, but it is the inevitable result of destroying the birds.

Remember that the plague of grasshoppers, so fearful at the West,
is attributed entirely by some persons to the reckless slaughter of the
prairie-hens shot by tens of thousands by covetous speculators, who
send them now to Europe.

Otsego Leaves II:
The Bird Mediæval

HERE AND THERE, in looking over old records or family legends of colonial years, the mediæval period of American story, we gather glimpses of bird-life, somewhat dim and indistinct, perhaps, yet sufficiently clear to have a degree of interest. We seem to hear the far-away flapping of wings, the echo of song; we have a vision, as it were, of the winged creatures flitting to and fro about the homes of the early colonists.

The Dutch were a race not unkindly in household life. Most of the country-homes of the Dutch colonists, whether your manor-house of some importance or the rude farmhouse of the yeoman, were peopled with merry black faces in-doors, while without, porch, garden, and yard, were favorite gathering-places for birds of many feathers. The negroes were great allies of the birds. Many were the ingenious devices of their own contrivance for enticing the little creatures to build about the dwelling which was their own home as well as that of their masters.

One pleasant afternoon in the later days of April, of a year far away, the huge doors of a large barn, not far from the bank of the Upper Hudson, stood open to their greatest width. It was a barn of which we have the actual measurement, more than a hundred feet long and sixty feet in breadth, the great doors being in the gable-end toward the river. An odd medley of sounds came through those great doors: voices old and young were chattering in broad negro Dutch—a gibberish somewhat harsh in itself, and yet softened by an unctuous slipping over of consonants, and spoken by voices untrained, but naturally musical. This was a holiday evening. It was Paas-week—Easter-tide. Paas was a grand holiday with the Dutch negroes. There had been a feast in the great barn at the Flats earlier in the day, and now the last of the rustic wreaths and rude benches were being carried away, and things set to rights again. Two negro matrons, of ample size, somewhat past middle age, were there directing matters, their heads covered with the bright kerchiefs in which the race delight, their broad figures and round faces now wearing an aspect of no little authority. Dianamat and Mariamat were, indeed, the queens of the kitchen, and that in good, patriarchal right, for, with one exception, they were mothers and grandmothers of the negro flock which made up the household, the solitary exception being an old, white-headed negro, "Uncle Cobus," formerly the factotum, now an abdicated dignitary. The sable dames were dowagers of no little importance. They knew the world. Had they not seen savage life in Africa in their early girlhood? And who, pray, should know so well the fashions of high burgher life in the great city of "All-bonny?"—a city, mind you, boasting two streets of some length, a fort, a Dutch and an English church, a wharf, and a fleet of a dozen sloops making weekly voyages to New York. Had they not cooked grand wedding-feasts and caudle-feasts, and, though last not least, funeral-feasts, in one of the stateliest homes in that renowned city for nearly half a century? These two great personages were allies, and yet rivals—a state of things by no means peculiar to a Dutch kitchen. They were close allies, with what they considered a Holy Alliance, where the interest or dignity of master or mistress was concerned. They were scolding rivals where the individual interest or dignity of child, grandchild, great-grandbaby, or favorite cow, or pet pig, was even remotely aimed at. On this particular afternoon, however, there was holiday harmony, *entente cordiale*, between these dusky dignitaries. The clearing of the barn, the picking up of any stray wooden platter, or horn spoon, or gourd dipper, this was the common aim of both; their stalwart sons, meanwhile, were carrying away rude benches and tables on their backs, and a troop of rollicking children were at wild and noisy gambols among the faded wreaths and blossoms. The vast, shadowy hay-loft above was nearly empty at that season, and the wealth of grain—wheat, rye, oats—which had filled the enormous chests below, had dwindled away under the demand for winter food and fodder. Now and then a hen would come out of the hay above and cackle over a newly-laid egg, or a cock perched on a bare pole gave a ringing brow of defiance to the fowls below, turkeys, ducks, and other poultry, who were picking up stray grains of oat, and wheat, and maize, or crumbs from the feast. There was a long row of stalls on each side of the broad barn-floor, telling of rich herds; in winter those stalls were filled with cows, oxen, and horses, their heads all turned toward the great thrashing-floor, but they were now mostly empty. Several cows, with young calves, were standing, or lying, in the stalls on either side; a couple of oxen were lazily chewing the cud of holiday idleness; and a lame horse was soberly taking his supper, apparently indifferent to the negro urchin perched on his back.

Wolf, when a half-grown colt, had once been attacked in a forest-pasture by a couple of wolves: one he kicked in the head and stunned; the other pursued him in hot chase through several fields into the very barn-yard, where the creature was killed with pitchforks. From that day the colt, a fine animal, bore the name of his enemy, and became, a year or two later, a favorite saddle-horse of the colonel. He was also often used for the carriage of madam. Now, Wolf was a very proud creature. He scorned the plough and the cart. Though docile as a saddle-horse, and taking pleasure apparently in being driven in his mistress's service, he became very unmanageable if he was brought out for work on the farm. He was very observant, and he was cunning, too. Whenever he saw Wout, or Tyte, or Brom, drawing the cart or plough into the foreground, and discovered that he was expected to do his share of work, he forthwith took to his heels, and generally succeeded in making his escape for the day. There was a large, half-wild island in the river, directly opposite the mansion-house, and this became a favorite refuge of Wolf in summer-time; whenever he shrewdly suspected that he would be needed in ploughing or harvesting, he

would leap over the gates, rush into the river, and swim across to the
island. There he had everything his own way—literally in clover the
live-long day. If he saw a boat coming after him, he would wait saucily
until it neared the shore, and then, kicking up his heels in defiance, he
would dash into the thicket, and lead his followers such a chase that
they were glad to give up the pursuit and return defeated to the barn-
yard. Toward sunset cunning Wolf would take a reconnaissance of the
state of things on the opposite bank: when he saw that the field-work,
and horses of more humble spirit, with the carts he hated, were moving
homeward, he would very coolly swim across the river again and walk
into the barn-yard, with a very hypocritical air, asking mutely for his
share of oats. He had recently been slightly lamed, and remained in the
stall this pleasant spring evening, receiving no little attention meanwhile from old and young. He was a sort of hero with the negroes,
but, then, every four-footed animal on the farm was the pet of some
one of the black people. Every creature had his especial friend and
champion, and wonderful were the stories they told of their favorites.

Now, with the animals, and the rollicking children, and the bustling
women, and the cackling poultry, the great barn was full of rustic
life and stir. And, good reader, amid all this movement, above all,
mingling with all, were the birds. Swallows were there by the half-
hundred, whirling, rising, falling, with the wonderful flight natural to
them, free and full of power, easy, graceful, noiseless. While seem-
ingly at idle play, weaving airy dances, the pretty creatures were, in
fact, busily at work building their odd, uncouth nests of mud, so rude
in aspect, so cunningly fashioned. To look at one of those mud-nests,
who could believe that it was to become the cradle of a creature so
purely aërial as the swallow? Seventy of those brown nests, many
old, others new, and still unfinished, might have been counted clinging to the vast, sloping roof, or clustering on the beams. In and out
through the great doors, in and out through smaller openings, high
over the roof without, low over the broad river beyond, in shadow
and sunshine, now grazing the heads of the noisy negroes, now glid-

ing over the quiet cattle in the stalls, now whirling among the doves and martins, which also haunted that vast, hospitable barn-roof, were the sprite-like swallow-people. Yes, the great barn was full of merry, cheery life, in which the negroes, old and young, filled the largest space, no doubt, but in which the birds far outnumbered them.

There was one quiet corner, however. Yonder on the floor sat a white-headed old negro, intent, apparently, on some small task of his own. What this quiet task was we shall see presently: it concerned the birds. Uncle Cobus, now an old man, was one of the dignitaries of the Flats. In his youth he had been a sort of genius, a clever Jack-of-all-trades, making canoes and paddles and nets; mending wheels and yokes; managing the fishing; working the cider-mill; breaking wild horses, and shoeing the tame ones; raising tobacco; raising flax and hemp, and moreover spinning both. But now Uncle Cobus was old; he pottered about the garden and poultry-yard in summer-time, and in winter sat in the warm kitchen, spinning, or cobbling old shoes for the household.

Presently, while Cobus was still at his task, those dignified personages, the heads of the family, colonel and madam, appeared at the barn-door—a tall and very stately couple they were, the gentleman elderly, erect, and slender, the lady middle-aged, tall, and stout. The colonel wore a sort of imitation of the costume in favor ten years earlier among men of his class in England—an imitation marked in many of its details by touches not only provincial but somewhat rustic. Madam was clad in garments chiefly of the finest homespun material, though the mantua of black silk had come from beyond the sea a dozen years earlier. On her head was a green-silk calash. There was little, indeed, of fashion about the cutting and trimming, but the dress was worn with a simple, womanly ease and dignity, which many a bedizened, overloaded fine lady of the present day might have envied. Two pretty little girls, near relatives and adopted children, accompanied the lady and gentleman, prattling together in Dutch. Their clothing was precisely like that of the negro children in the barn—homespun in fabric, but finer in quality and neater in condition. To modern eyes they would have looked like two little old women, full of fun and play. Each wore, with an air of mischief, a large, battered man's hat.

The colonel and madam had come to see Wolf, and they had also come to see a hawk of unusual size killed a day or two earlier. Wolf was visited, caressed, and fed with maple-sugar, by the little girls. The cows, calves, and oxen, all received their share of kindly attention. And then came the turn of the hawk.

"What have you done with your hawk, Wout?" asked the colonel—in Dutch, of course—speaking to the stout negro in Wolf's stall.

"Nailed him up on the door of the poultry-house," was Wout's reply. Would master like to see him?—the biggest hawk that had been killed on the farm for ten years; the same old rascal who had carried off so many chickens and ducklings and turkey-poults—they knew him by his bigness. He was so cunning and so swift of wing that, until now, he had escaped unhurt, though shot at twenty times.

Wout, you see, was not a little proud of his feat as a marksman.

Yes, the colonel and madam wished to see this famous hawk; and they moved toward the poultry-yard at their usual leisurely, dignified pace—a large following of chattering negroes of all sizes at their heels. That yard, in the rear of the kitchen, was oddly peopled. The various pets of the negroes were living there in rude cages—two or three squirrels, a musk-rat, a tame beaver, and, what was considered its chief ornament, a young bear's cub, daintily fed on honey and fruits whenever those could be obtained. These pets from the wilderness were all very important members of the household, a great delight to their different owners. There were a number of birds, in cages also, housed in winter, but now hanging out in the spring sunshine; all were native birds—crow, robin, a couple of yellow-birds, blue-bird, and red-winged blackbird. And yonder, on the farther side of the yard, nailed to the door of the poultry-yard, with outstretched wings, was the hawk. It was, indeed, a large bird, about four feet in breadth from one wing-tip to the other, and some twenty-two inches in length. This

same white-breasted hawk had carried off a hen from the poultry-yard
a month earlier—a hen whose young chicks had to be brought up under the wing of Dianamat instead of the maternal feathers.

It was still what might be called early spring in that region in the first
days of April. The return of the birds of passage was always closely
watched by the negroes, after the long, silent winter, and that interest
was still at its height. Many black hands had been busy of late preparing accommodations for the winged people. The sheds and the rear
of the kitchen were well garnished with a quaint array of old hats,
these being considered as especially tempting lodgings for the birds.
In a trice, madam's little *protégées* were bareheaded, and the two old
battered, mouse-nibbled, moth-eaten hats they had discovered in the
garret were nailed up by Wout for the service of some wren or blue-
bird. Besides a dozen of these old hats, there were one or two cracked
gourds, or squash-shells, and several rudely-built bird-houses doing
duty in the same way. And in the centre of the yard was a large pollard-
tree, whose limbs had been cut off at midsummer years before when
full of sap, every decayed branch leaving in time a hole in the trunk,
of which the birds soon took possession. The little creatures, indeed,
might have considered themselves as lords of the manor—they built
their nests wherever they fancied, on bush or shrub, low in the grass,
high in the tallest tree, under the eaves, on the window-sills, in the
garret, in the chimneys, in the barns and sheds, in the old hats, in the
pollard-tree. They seemed to know that they were at home at the Flats,
where every one made them welcome.

The chattering negroes had much to say about the little bird-fam-
ilies already in possession of tree or hat, while many more were expected. The previous summer the garden had been honored by the
presence of a mocking-bird and his mate, who built in a pear-tree. This
was a rare event. Seldom had those noble songsters been heard at the
Flats, though not uncommon at that date near New York. And one of
the stories old Cobus was fond of telling at the chimney-corner related
to the visit of a flock of lovely green paroquets, which had amazed

the Dutch farmers and their negroes, some years earlier, by visiting the banks of the Mohawk. They were beautiful green birds, smaller but handsomer, according to Uncle Cobus, than the solitary parrot in "All-bonny," which was a sort of family connection, belonging to a niece of madam.

But where was old Cobus all this time, and what was he about? We shall see if we follow the troop of holiday people as they return again to the great barn, headed by the colonel and madam. There, on the floor, sat the old man. Do not think harshly of him, I beg, when I tell you that Uncle Cobus sat in the midst of a row of—skulls! Let us hasten to observe that they were not human skulls; they were the skeleton heads of horses, cows, and oxen, once inhabitants of the Great Barn. The old negro had been busy putting what he considered finishing touches to these skulls, cleansing them within, scraping them without, until each had assumed an appropriate aspect of ghastly whiteness. The colonel and madam looked down upon these strange objects complacent and indulgent. They were evidently well accustomed to similar sights. Pointing with his cane to one of the skulls, the colonel asked if that was not the head of Blackbird, a famous ox. Yes; he had guessed aright—so said Uncle Cobus. Dianamat and Mariamat then came forward, and, each holding up the skull of a favorite cow, began fondling them tenderly with those fat, black hands of theirs, singing the praises of Bonnyclabber and White Clover—where should they see the like of those cows?—so many quarts at a milking, such cream, such butter, such cheese! This horse's head had belonged to the mate of Wolf, killed the previous year by an accident; that was a colt from which much had been expected. Not a skull on the floor but the negroes knew to which of their fellow-workers on the farm it had belonged. The old man had now finished his task. Rising to his feet, he took up the head of the famous ox, while the women and children, Wout and Tyte, seized upon others, and each, as it were, hugging a skull in his arms, all moved toward the barn-door in a sort of informal procession, the colonel and madam bringing up the rear. This somewhat striking,

not to say imposing, procession took up its march through the barn-
yard, then through orchard, garden, and meadow, until it reached the
boundary of the grounds in that direction. Beyond, on the bank of the
river, ran the highway, the great northern route from Albany, aiming,
somewhat blindly, at Canada, but, in fact, going little beyond a very
rude settlement, some twenty miles distant, called Saratoga. The highway and river-bank were shaded in summer by elms and sycamores,
magnificent in growth, luxuriant in foliage, and festooned with grape-
vines and creepers; below ran the great river, full to the brim with half
the melted snows of the Adirondack valleys. The whitewashed fence,
bounding the farm toward the highway, was the goal of the sable procession. This fence from its public position was supposed to need especial attention; every spring it was carefully whitewashed by Uncle
Cobus, and, this annual whitewashing being now over, it was about to
receive other improvements. The nature of the proposed ornamenta-
tion might be gathered from that already bestowed upon it. Every post
supporting this fence was crowned with a skull! Every dead animal belonging to the farm whose skull was sufficiently large for the purpose
was honored with a post. And they were many. The herds were large,
and the fence of some length: if the number of skeleton heads was not
sufficiently great at any time, others were begged or borrowed from
the adjoining farms of the colonel's brothers, Pedrom and Jeremias.
Very proud were Uncle Cobus, and Tyte, and Wout, and Dianamat,
and Mariamat, of this savage array. Did it not show how many cows
had grazed in their meadows; how many stately horses master had
owned? All skulls which had been in any way injured during the past
winter, by accident or by the wear and tear of storm and time, were
now removed, and others put in their places. Many were the tender associations connected with these remains of the four-footed friends and
comrades of the negroes. Even the children knew the names of many
of these skeletons by heart; as for Mariamat and Dianamat, they occasionally visited this fence solely for the purpose of reviving mournful
recollections of deceased queens of the herd. One skull was especially

honored; it was that of Annetje, named after Queen Anne of blessed memory, having been imported from England in her reign.

Each skull was carefully and firmly placed on the post, with the jaws downward. There was a purpose in this. It was for the benefit of the birds that this was done. There was, indeed, a double motive in this array of white skeleton heads; they were intended quite as much for bird-homes as for the adornment of the fence. In most of the skulls already in position there were nests of the previous year's building. And in those Uncle Cobus and Wout were now placing on the posts there would ere long be merry wrens or shy blue-birds flitting in and out through the sockets of the skeleton eyes. They had a fancy for building in the crania of these skulls, a fancy the negroes had observed and encouraged. The little creatures seemed to feel themselves very much at home in those grim dwellings. They would fly in and out, utterly careless of observation. From prowling cat or curious child they were, indeed, perfectly safe. And woe betide the negro urchin who should try bird-nesting among that ghastly row of skeleton heads, the pride of the Flats!

Otsego Leaves III:
The Bird Primeval

AN ANCIENT TREE of great height, a grand old column of the wilderness, stood rooted on a hill-side, overlooking a highland lake. The tree was an elm. The lake lay in the heart of a forest of varied growth, where oak, maple, chestnut, elm, ash, hickory, were blended with the evergreen pine and fir. The same forest stretched in one unbroken canopy a hundred leagues to the eastward, where it met the Ocean. Toward the setting sun it seemed boundless to the few human beings who, at that remote period, wandered among its shadows. It was a vast wilderness, full of mysteries. And much of the mystery of that leafy wilderness can never be revealed to human ken.

History, as belonging to that period of the hemisphere, is a grand, grave, wild figure, gazing earnestly backward, with the reflection of a wonderful vision in its far-seeing eyes. How much could she tell us that we are longing to know, how many marvels could she unfold that we are craving to inquire into! But never a word shall she utter. Hers is a sublime vision, sweeping over a vast continent, and including a past of thousands of years. But she is mute—utterly mute—mute forever. Silence is her doom.

The history of a wilderness, if entirely accurate—the long record of a savage race, if strictly true—might indeed be of very high import to the civilized world of to-day. How much of practical truth, precious in its lessons, might be learned from those unwritten scrolls! But they are never to be read. All records north of Mexico, save a few dim outlines on the rock, have perished with the pictured roll of birch-bark.

Nevertheless, it is a glimpse into this vast wilderness that we are about to offer you, good reader. And we shall tell you nothing but what is true. Our little sketch shall be correct in its outlines at least. The red-man, and all the larger animals who haunted that region a thousand years ago, have passed away, have vanished almost entirely. But the trees of that grand forest, and the birds who haunted them, are here to-day. Yes, the trees, with the wild blossoms—tender, modest, fragrant, growing at their roots—and the birds haunting that vast world of branches, are nearly all that remain to us of that period of mysteries.

The ancient elm we have chosen to sketch for you had looked over the mountain-lake, and its setting of hill and forest, for three hundred years. The tall, gray column, perfectly erect, without a break in the line for seventy feet, and standing on a projecting knoll, commanded a view of half the lake and its closely-wooded shores. Those ancient trees of forest growth had a peculiar character: the stately column was generally bare of branch or twig, colored each with its own peculiar shade of gray, and marked here and there perchance with the scar left by a limb fallen perhaps a century earlier, or stained with slowly gathering patches of moss and lichen. The general tint, however, with the elm was a clear gray, the accident of scar or lichen scarcely showing at a little distance. And the lines in the bark, less deep and rugged than those of some other trees, ran upward with more of regularity and accurate tracery. Like all its comrades of the same age, all who had battled with storm and tempest for centuries, this old elm could show nothing of verdure, save a crown on its lofty summit. Strange that the elm, a tree so peculiarly graceful in the sweep of its branches, so luxuriant in delicate spray and foliage, and often, when growing in the freedom of lawn or meadow, partially feathered with verdure to the root, should have stood thus stern and bare when standing in the ancient forest. But the general character of the individual trees making up that vast wilderness was touched with something of a savage aspect, differing widely from the forest of civilization. The hand of man leaves its impress of culture even on the woods of a thickly-peopled country. In the ancient wilderness, the trees seemed to reflect something of the nature of the savage hunting within their shadows. The summits of all the mountains and highlands of the Northern Alleghanies were crowned at that period with a crest of evergreen pinnacles, formed by the towering growth of the white-pine, rising in stern array some fifty feet above the tallest oak and elm. There was something singularly wild in the expression of those tall and aged pines of the wilderness, unbending, and scantily clothed with whorls of short evergreen branches toward their summits. There were many such standing near the old elm, and rising far above it, but from its accidental position on the projecting knoll, and from the fact that a windrow had made a partial breach among the trees immediately below, a bird perched on its highest branch could look far away over wood and water.

Half the lofty crown of this aged elm had been torn away by a crashing storm of thunder and lightning some fifty summers earlier. Branch and twig had fallen, and a great rift had been made in the trunk for some twenty feet from the summit. The old elm was now a half-shattered ruin; the tuft of branches still coming into leaf in the spring sunshine was becoming more meagre with every passing summer. Gray stag-horns appeared among its fresh leaves, even when the wild-roses were in bloom. The highest of those gray and leafless branches was a lookout-station, well known to crow and blue-jay, born and bred, and passing their lives, in the adjoining forest. Many birds have a fancy for those high and naked limbs, whence they can look down at their leisure upon the lower world.

An experienced old crow now sat upon the blighted bough, looking lazily over the forest, stretching far away north and south, and toward the setting sun. Not one human habitation could his dark hazel eye discover on the shores. Not a single faint column of smoke rose from the forest. Not a solitary skiff on the lake, which lay placid and smiling in the sunlight with a sweetness and freshness which would seem to belong to those limpid waters in the early awakening of spring, after their

long winter's slumber. Hill and forest were clearly reflected in delicate
tracery on that opal-like mirror, and at that moment the picture was
one of varied shading—here a broad belt of dark evergreen, yonder a
reach of light-gray tracery touched here and there with tender green
or the red or yellowish tassels of the maples, or the snow-like bloom
of the amelanchier and wild-plum. Many of the trees, however, were
still thoroughly gray.

To the southward, and at no great distance, a young river flowed
from the lake, and, winding onward with increase of breadth as it
traveled over a long path to the Ocean, soon became one of the great
water-arteries of the region. But human eye, when looking toward the
south from the knoll, would have sought in vain to follow its track.
The sharp-eyed crow saw nothing in that direction but interlacing
bough and twig, either dark green or light gray. Even at that hour,
when half the forest was still bare of leaf, not a single gleam of sunlight revealed the stream gliding silently beneath the forest-arch. And
at no point, even on that bright spring morning, could human eye have
penetrated to the leafy bed of the forest in looking down from the hill-
side. The face of the earth was closely veiled. Opening in the forest
there was none. Here and there a windrow had overthrown a group
of the old trees; and there was one such, as we have said, immediately
below the knoll, but there was nothing to be seen at that point but a
wild, confused mass of prostrate giants of the forest or their upheaved
roots, or shattered limbs. It was a record of some past tempest in singular contrast with the general aspect of the woods at that moment, so
still and peaceful in the hopeful calm of early spring.

There was but little air playing among the gray branches or the
tender, opening leaves. Even the mysterious murmurs among the
old pines could scarcely be heard. Occasionally the note of a single
bird rose from the forest. The old crow had come over the lake, with
heavily-flapping wing, crying "Caw! caw!" as he alighted on the dead
branch. But he was silent now. The solitary note of a red-breasted
robin, or song-sparrow, or the tap of a woodpecker, might be heard

perchance at intervals. There was a dreamy silence pervading the highland forest, even on that soft spring morning. The life and the movement of the land seemed at that moment to belong to the birds alone, as they flitted silently to and fro among the trees. There were, however, wild creatures, large and fierce, lying slumbering at that sun-shiny hour in shallow cave, or dark ravine, or crouching among fallen timber.

About the old elm there was more of winged life and movement than elsewhere on the mountain-side, but it was a noiseless life. One by one small, dark birds of a dull-brown color came wheeling above the old crow, their long wings and short bodies darting through the air with wonderful rapidity, and with scarcely a vibration of the wings, whirling, diving, darting to and fro, and vanishing, as it were, one by one, each diving with a singular rapidity and precision into the heart of the old elm. That aged trunk was hollow for some fifty feet downward from the open rift above. At the height of a man from the root it would have required three stalwart savage hunters to embrace the trunk in its outward girth. Within, the hollow space, at its widest point, measured twice the length of a man's arm in diameter. The en-tire hollow column was crowded with those singular birds, and had been their summer-house for half a century. They were now building new nests or repairing those of earlier years. And busy workers they were, only occasionally soaring away into the upper air for an hour of play and pleasure, or in search of food. They rose far above the tallest pines in easy, graceful flight, rising, falling, darting to and fro with scarcely a vibration of the wings, and then, floating over the lake in airy dance, would seem at times to graze the waters. Never were they seen to alight for a brief rest, or to feed, or to sing, like other birds. Their ways were entirely different. They lived on the wing. And they were silent creatures: song they had none—their sole speech was a faint, twittering sound, heard occasionally. At the hour when the old crow had alighted on his favorite perch, few were abroad. It was in early morning and in the evening that these dusky people were most active. Many of them were now clinging, with their muscular feet and long and very sharp hooked claws, to the inner surface of the hollow trunk, using the strong shafts of their tails also for support, and, with their short, black bills for tools, were building the cradles for their young. After their fashion, these cradles were skillfully put together. They were made of slender twigs rudely interlaced, a sort of little basket, small and shallow, and the twigs were cemented together by a copious supply of gum or mucilage secreted in the stomachs of the little builders. These basket-nests had no lining whatever. They were secured to the inner surface of the tree by the cement of natural mucilage. If a twig was needed, the bird rose into the air and floated silently away, shooting swiftly to and fro, amusing himself perchance for a moment by a winged dance with some companion, but sure to return after a while with the needed bit of twig. And where, pray, did he find the tiny branch? Was it picked up while flying low over the bed of the forest? Have you ever seen this dull-colored but most active creature collect his building-materials? I trow not. Other birds, in forest or meadow, in garden or on lawn, are often seen gathering the materials out of which they build their nests. It is one of the pleasures of spring to watch them. Any day, early in the season, you may chance to see blue-bird, phœbe, wren, alight on the ground, and pick up a withered blade of grass, a tiny straw, a bit of string, or a hair from horse or cow, and fly away to secret haunts of their own. The robin is often very bold and very pertinacious in his quest for materials; he may be seen tugging away, for half an hour at a time, at some obstinate bit of twine which he has partially loosened from the flower-bed, and, if not successful, he will return again and again. If you step out when he is away, and cut the twine for him, he will be very much obliged to you, and he will be sure to carry it off. Both the sober robin and the brilliant oriole will carry away what would seem an inconvenient load for their bills on these occasions. An oriole has been known to carry off a good-sized skein of thread, and, moreover, weave it skillfully into its pendulous nest. And, a while ago, a robin built his nest very boldly, within sight and within reach, out of long, narrow cuttings of wall-paper, which had been thrown into the rubbish-barrel after papering a room; he seemed to take pride in the use of this new material, for he so arranged it that many of these long streamers were left floating from beneath his nest all summer. And it was but the other day I sat watching another robin daintily collecting, one by one, quite a little sheaf of fine, short shreds of withered grass; the skill with which he picked up one, without dropping the others, was amusing, and he carried them all off in his bill, at the same time giving me a look half saucy, half shy, as he flew away. Occasionally, if you are resting quietly in the woods some early spring-day, you may chance to see a pretty and rare sight: a humming-bird poised with quivering wing before an odd-looking object, a rather uncouth, brown, woolly ball, uncouth now, but soon to unfold into the graceful frond of fern; little ruby-throat will pluck off a scrap of this brown, woolly down of the fern and carry it away to help line his nest. But if you see this you are in luck—it is a rare sight, for ruby-throat is very sly and mysterious at building-time. And unless you are a favored mortal, you are not likely to see a swallow gathering his little fagot of twigs—the sole materials of his nest. Do the birds then gather them from the bed of the forest? Do they pick them up while skimming over the water? Do the swifts find these twigs in the clouds? Who can tell? They are wonderful creatures. They are at home in the sky—they feed, and dance, and play, and twitter, and swim, in the air—the earth they *never* touch! From the moment they break the shell, and have learned to ply their wings, to the last spark of life, they belong to the trees and the air solely. This gleaning of twigs for building becomes, therefore, a mystery to common mortals. The old crow, however, shall solve the riddle for you. He has seen this little brown creature peering round among the trees until he finds a small dead twig suited to his purpose, but still attached to the parent-branch; this he seizes with his feet—feet utterly useless for walking, but strong with muscular power, and armed with claws admirable for clinging—and with these strong feet and sharp claws the bird succeeds in breaking the twig, which is borne swiftly away to the new nest, placed in position, and well secured by the cement from his own bill.

More than half a hundred of these rude basket-nests made up the nursery in the old elm. The building was not a long process. Eggs then appeared in each—four pretty little white eggs. It would seem as if those dusky creatures should lay brown or speckled eggs. But it is not so. The eggs were white. And ere long out of those white shells came a small multitude of uncouth fledglings, blind as bats, and not a little bat-like in aspect. And great was now the din within the old tree, when the little creatures opened their short bills for food: to and fro, high and low, the parent-birds now glided through the air in quest of the insect game required by their family. Little fathers and mothers, a hundred or more, knew no rest; repose was vanished from the heart of the riven elm. The old crow had no peace; he was often driven away from his perch by the sheer force of numbers rushing to and fro. The birds never attacked him, for they are harmless, peaceable creatures, and, though somewhat timid and shy, would yet appear to have such confidence in their own powers of wing that they will often dart dangerously near a deadly enemy. The crow was an enemy. We must confess the fact. He would greatly have enjoyed a feast of those white eggs. Do not blame him; you like an egg for breakfast yourself, do you not? And he would gladly have dined off a few of the young ones also; another point of resemblance between crow and man, although you would doubtless have preferred something more plump than those scrawny cousins to the bats, and you would scarcely have eaten them *au naturel*, as the crow was sure to do whenever he had a chance. Probably one object of his frequent visits to the dead limb of that old elm was to watch for a chance to pick up a bird now and then. He had an old wife—your crow is a sensible creature, he knows the value of a life-long companionship, he mates for life—and a nest full of dark children in the neighborhood. He must seek provision for them. Very seldom was he successful, however, and only in the case of some careless young one. The older birds defied him by their marvelous swiftness.

At this period of hatching and feeding, there was a perpetual din— a dull murmur heard from within the hollow tree. These most silent of birds, silent and songless in voice, noiseless in flight, now produced a strange, mysterious sound, the effect of the unceasing movement of the anxious, little winged parents, watching and feeding their nurslings. Their activity seemed to redouble at this moment. Scarcely a minute passed when food was not brought in by some one of the birds. They flew far and wide in quest of it, and yet were at home again in a trice. One of the attractions of the old elm, in the eyes of the bird-colony, was its nearness to the lake below; they loved to float over the water, drinking as they flew, and their choicest insect-game was found hovering over the lake and river, in little dancing flocks. For a clumsy bear it might have been perhaps a fifteen minutes' walk down the wild, steep hill-side to the shore. But in a few seconds the swift was there, disporting himself joyously. At favorable moments in the early morning, at evening hours, and in cloudy, showery days, he met there many companions of his own kind whirling in graceful maze to and fro. And other feathered creatures were afloat on the water. Ducks of many feathers were swimming, rising, falling, in little parties of their own, among them lovely wood-ducks, nesting in trees overhanging the lake.

There were reaches of the shore where the limpid waters were shallow, rolling over a clean bottom of pebbles, and here white, branchless trunks of ancient trees could plainly be seen lying where they had fallen headlong into the lake, weakened by centuries of age, or laid low by the tempest. Other fallen giants of the old forest, still branching at their summits, and touched here and there with verdure, had also dropped from the bank, but were only partially submerged, though reaching, perhaps, thirty feet into the lake; on these half-submerged wrecks of trees young saplings had grown up, vines and creepers clung to them, and a few wild-flowers bloomed among the moss, on the half-

decayed trunks, the whole forming a fantastic little point stretching
out from the shore here and there. It was near one of these leafy points
that the swallows frequently saw a few noble birds floating grandly to
and fro, entirely white in plumage, silent, majestic in movement, with
long, graceful necks, and black bills. They were swans, whose nests
lay in a marshy spot on the shore. Seldom on the wing, the beautiful
forms of those brilliant white birds often gleamed in the sunlight on the
blue water. And there were other great water-fowl still larger than the
swan, with white plumage tinged with pinkish red, frequently in sight
near a low point on the western shore, where they had their nests; they
were heavy and uncouth in movement, bearing a large bill and great
pouch beneath it; these were the large white pelicans, rarely in flight,
often in drowsy sleep on the water.

Nor was it only feathered creatures that the swallows saw in their
flight over the lake. Often they flitted over the heads of the graceful
deer, or the large elk, lapping the water in morning and evening hours.
Not unfrequently the tall, dark, ungainly moose was there also, up-
rooting the water-lilies, or feeding daintily on the buds of the wild-
roses growing along the shore. With a colony of beavers also they
were on visiting terms, so far, at least, as making flying calls to the
beaver-town at a point on the opposite shore. These primeval swallows saw, indeed, many sights which your civilized modern eyes shall
never behold.

Nay, they saw more than most creatures haunting the shores of
the same forest-lake. They were on the wing more than most birds.
The sun found them hovering over the water when he arose above the
eastern hill, and he left them there when, after the long summer day,
he dropped slowly to the westward. There was scarcely an hour in
the night when a few of those anxious father and mother birds were
not roving over the water, hunting among the night-moths great and
small. There was feeding going on in the old elm, more or less, all
through the night. A dull, rumbling sound like distant thunder was often heard in the darkness, as well as in daylight hours, from within the

riven tree. Many a graceful deer, passing near the elm, would suddenly pause in listening attitude, startled by that mysterious sound. Was it a pack of wolves in pursuit? Perchance, indeed, the cruel wolves were not far away, and were rushing on the track of the stag as he leaped through the wood, seeking the lake-shore. The ungainly bear, who had wintered in a cave not far to the southward, would also pause to listen in his night wandering, near the hollow tree, and perchance he would paw the trunk in inquiring wonder. The wily panther, coming and going on errands of his own, haunting the cliffs to the northward, would hear the rumbling from the heart of the old tree, and crawl with stealthy movement, and glaring, cruel eye, to the root of the great elm to listen. Strange, is it not, that birds who have so little voice, whose only speech is a faint twitter, whose airy flight is so easy, so noiseless, should thus produce this subdued roar within an old tree? It was the constant movement of the parent-birds feeding their young, coming and going through the hollow column which sheltered their flock, that produced the busy murmur.

And this movement, whether under sunshine or moonlight, went on through the midsummer weeks. There were two sets of little white eggs laid in many of those rude basket-nests; two broods of odd little fledglings clinging to the inner surface of the tree. But ere long the whole nursery, elder and younger birds, was afloat in the air, the flock being nearly quadrupled in numbers since the arrival of the parent-birds in the spring. Then came a general holiday—a merry, joyous, dancing time. They were abroad all day in idle pleasuring, high, high in the air, far above the grandest pines, low over the lake, where they now saw the young, blue-gray cygnets swimming about their proud mother, and the odd, ash-colored young pelicans, with those uncouth bills and pouches.

During the day the great elm was now deserted. Old Crow came back to his favorite perch unmolested. But at night, about sunset, the whole swallow-flock would whirl and flutter about the riven tree, and then vanish within to roost for the night.

The weather was still very warm. The later summer flowers were coming into bloom. The berries were ripening in the woods. The air was full of insect-life. The whole forest was richly green. At this very period of the season, when the luxuriant affluence of summer was still unfading, there came an evening when the old crow sat preening his feathers on the blighted branch in perfect solitude. Not a single swallow returned! The old riven elm was deserted. The movement and murmur within the giant trunk had utterly ceased! And whither, pray, had the swallows gone? They were sailing through the air far to the southward, feeding on choice insect-game as they floated over immense tracts of forest, made up of trees grand and ancient, but somewhat differing from those about the highland lake where these swift creatures had been hatched. They passed over the valleys of broad rivers. Here and there they beheld bands of savage men tricked out in feathers and paint. They saw the wary hunter armed with bow and arrow. They heard the war-whoop. They reached a vast gulf of a silent Ocean. They soared over a sailless sea. They beheld a fleet of gay canoes. They reached a low, watery region, and here they met millions of their kind. Here, also, they saw men of a semi-civilized race—men who built temples and palaces of stone; men alike in color, in stature, in many personal details, yet differing widely in habits and modes of life from the few wild hunters which visited the home-lake of the swifts.

And why, then, had they left that remote highland lake at a moment when its shores were still in their full summer glory, when the sun was still brilliant and warm, when the air was teeming with insect-life? Why had they traveled over half a continent to reach that low, hot country? That is indeed a mystery which neither crow nor writer can solve. The crow, indeed, may have thought their flight a folly, for he passed all his life, summer and winter, on the shores of that forest-lake. There was no month in the year when he had not perched on that dead limb of the riven elm. Nevertheless, the active swifts had, no doubt, very good reasons of their own for their long flight to the southward. And now the old gray column of the wilderness stood lonely and deserted—a ruined tower, abandoned by the hundreds of winged creatures born within its sheltering walls.

A thousand summers, good reader, have come and gone since that period. A thousand generations of those dusky little birds have fluttered over the same lake. And the latest of those thousand generations is with us to-day, still floating over tree and water. But if you look for them in the woods you will look in vain—you will not find them. They no longer haunt the forest. Not one shall you find building a basket-nest in a hollow tree! The village grown up on the lake shore is now their home. They are weaving their airy dance this evening over your own roof; they are dropping one by one into your own chimneys!

A Lament for the Birds

IN THE COUNTRY about the head-waters of the Susquehanna the hills were all crowned some forty years since with a stern crest of spearlike pines, living and dead, rising to a great height above the lower wood. (Those wild old pines have now nearly all fallen from the heights about Lake Otsego.) The living trees still showed a scanty foliage, in irregular whorls, colored with the dark emerald-green of the white pine. Many others were mere gray skeletons, ghosts of trees as it were, destroyed by forest fires of the past, but still erect in death. It is surprising how long a pine of the white species will preserve its original form without a trace of life at its heart, though rocked perchance by the storms of half a century. To-day the same hills show the rounded sky-line of the younger wood, especially so in summer, when all the trees are in full leaf. The tall old pines have fallen beneath the axe.

If there were tongues in trees, as the poet would fain have us believe, those wild old pines could have told us a strange tale of bird life connected with the past.

The great white pelican, largest of water-fowls, may very possibly have floated on this lake in far-away years. This bird, majestic in size, beautiful in white plumage, awkward in movement, uncouth in form from its enormous pouch, has had in the Old World a long history, veiled in myth. On this continent it is said to have frequented inland lakes and rivers in preference to the coast. We may fancy it, if we choose, as lingering about some wooded point of the Otsego water, its nest shaded by the wild rose and azalea of a past century. The flint arrow-head we picked up yesterday among the gravel on the

lake shore may have been aimed at the great pelican by some Mohawk
hunter of the dark ages of this region.

The beautiful white swan has no doubt floated on Lake Otsego.
This graceful bird, partial to inland waters, still builds its nest in the
Adirondack country, where there are very many lakes and tarns. The
Alleghanies proper, though boasting of grand rivers, can show but few
lakes. One of the most northern of these is Lake Otsego. Beyond all
doubt the white swan has visited these waters in years not very remote.

But leaving the mysteries of the past, half fact, half fable, we reach
the early years of the present century. From this date we have a clear
record of bird life. There have been great changes among the feathered
tribes within that period.

Very remarkable has been the history of the native wild-pigeon, a
bird entirely peculiar to North America, from the Gulf of Mexico to
Hudson Bay. Its history is not only very interesting, but quite wonderful in some of its details. The bird itself, taken singly, as we rus-
tics know, is elegant in form, and very pleasing in its slate-colored
plumage, tinged with a pale shading of red on the breast. It is very gentle and peaceable, entirely harmless, and even timid by nature. Who
would have thought it possible that gentle birds like these should have
swept over the interior of the continent within a century in flocks so
vast as to obscure the sun at noon as though the country lay under
an eclipse, while the ceaseless rapid motion of millions of wings produced a loud roar like an approaching tornado? Accurate and experienced men of science—Wilson and Audubon—tell us of vast flocks
covering 180 square miles of country in Kentucky as recently as 1813.
They tell us of vast breeding-places in Western forests many miles
in extent, where ninety nests were counted in one tree. They tell us
of roosting-grounds forty miles in length, with a breadth of several
miles, the uproar from this roosting-ground being heard at a distance
of three miles. They tell us of one column of these birds in flight covering 240 miles of country in length!

Grand indeed must have been the movement over the continent of that vast living winged cloud, a great marvel of nature. Nothing to equal it has been known elsewhere on earth.

The old pines on the hill-tops about the Otsego water some forty years since must have been frequently overshadowed by flocks of the wild-pigeon, much less wonderful than those farther west, but still remarkable in their numbers.

On the early morning of June 8, 1847, the lake and the village lay shrouded in a summer mist. A large flock of wild-pigeons became bewildered in the fog, and lost their way—an unusual incident in their history. Instinct failed to guide them. Their naturally keen sight could not pierce the mist. They dropped on the nearest trees, in the heart of the village, on our own lawn, in the church-yard, in the gardens, and on the elms and maples shading the streets. With the first rays of the sun appearing above Mount Vision the mist rose, the birds took flight.

In the early spring of 1849 a large flock of pigeons, supposed to number several thousands, selected for their breeding-ground a wood in the valley of the Susquehanna some miles to the southward of the lake. The details were similar to those reported of the vast breeding-places at the West—nests carelessly built of twigs, a number in close neighborhood in the same tree; broken limbs of trees; a low murmur of wings. But the ground occupied was a narrow one.

Since those years no large flocks of wild-pigeons have passed over Lake Otsego. A few only have been seen where formerly they were numbered by the hundred. To-day you inquire if any wild-pigeons have been recently found in these woods. *"None that we have seen or heard of lately,"* shall be the answer to your inquiry. What a change within forty years! Alas for the vanished wild-pigeon!

But the record of many other familiar birds formerly seen in cheerful flocks about this valley, though less tragic than that of the wild-pigeon, is still a sad one.

To those who are so happy as to have a permanent home in the country the birds fluttering about our doors and windows so cheerfully enter into the pleasures—nay, one may say into the joys—of daily life. But here again sad have been the changes within the last forty years.

The friendly red-breasted robins, the beautiful blue-birds, the gay musical goldfinches, those charming song-birds the wrens, the gorgeous orioles, the purple finches, the dainty greenlets, the pretty cedar-birds, the merry gold-crests, and their cousins the ruby-crowns, those dainty sprites the humming-birds—these and other bird families never failed in past years to bring joy with them to our lawns and meadows. Many of them are now rare visitors. The sturdy robins are much less numerous than they were formerly.

And even in winter days the merry chicadees and their more sober companions, the gray snow-birds, were sure to appear in flocks about our doors. To-day we may watch for these little friends of ours week after week, often disappointed, when perchance we may see three or four of the little creatures, who formerly came to us in pleasant companies.

There is less change among the swallow tribe than among other birds. Both the chimney-swallows and the barn-swallows are still seen hovering in large parties about our village homes and the barns of the country-side. These swallows are both peculiarly American birds. The sober uncouth-looking chimney-swallow is sure to come wheeling in graceful flight about our roofs in late April days. Though uncouth in form and very awkward in movement when on their feet, their flight is singularly rapid and graceful; it is a delight to watch them as they wheel over river and lake. The pretty barn-swallows, with their steel-blue backs and bright chestnut breasts, are still faithful visitors to our farms—gentle, friendly creatures, sweeping in graceful flight over highway and meadow, often taking pleasure in alighting in gay parties on the telegraph wires. Before houses were built on the lake shore our dusky friends the chimney-swallows lived in hollow trees in the forest, as those old pines could have told you. Before barns were built the pretty blue and chestnut swallows had a few nests in the shallow caves of these limestone hills. To-day both tribes have become civilized; they have entirely deserted the woods.

In autumn days, after the swallows have taken flight, few indeed are the birds now left to cheer us. Formerly large flocks of busy robins were often seen feasting on the berries of the mountain-ash, or the haws of the white-thorn about our homes. To-day on the same lawn you shall probably see only three or four redbreasts together as rare visitors. Frequently, forty years since, as you passed along a country road in early autumn you were accompanied by gay flocks gathering for their annual flight, but lingering to enjoy the last pleasant days, and feeding on the seeds of the wild plants by the road-side. Twenty merry goldfinches were seen on such an afternoon as they clustered in eager company on a single tall thistle. To-day you are in luck if you see three or four of these birds on some road-side weed.

After the bright autumn leaves of those years had all dropped from the trees, it was a pleasant habit to walk about the village streets and note the deserted nests in elm or maple. Frequently there were two, three, and occasionally even four and five nests in the same tree. To-day you may perhaps discover one or two nests in a dozen trees.

Again in winter days, after the first heavy fall of snow, it was a pleasure to watch from your windows the deserted nests of the larger birds crowned with a beautiful rounded cap of pure white. Often from one window half a dozen of these snow-crowned nests could be seen on the nearer trees. Last winter, among the many trees shading a village lawn, there was but one solitary snow-crowned nest in sight.

Alas for the vanished birds!

Emendations

A Dissolving View

5.6	blue-jays	blue jays
10.30	Renaissance	renaissance
16.4	lake shore	lake-shore

Introduction to *Country Rambles*

17.7	"Journal	Journal
17.8	Naturalist"	Naturalist
17.8	"Selborne,"	Selborne,
17.20	"The	The
17.20	Selborne,"	Selborne,
17.20	"Journal	Journal
17.20	Naturalist,"	Naturalist,
18.16	towns	town
22.18	affections.	affections

Introduction to *The Rhyme and Reason of Country Life*

24.20	no more	more
28.15	is	are
38.23	it	its
39.30	refreshment	refeshment
43.9	conceive	conceive that

Preface to the 1868 *Rural Hours*

45.24	Susquehanna	Susquehannah
45.25	lake shore	lake-shore

Later Hours

48.16	"Journal	Journal
48.16	Naturalist,"	Naturalist,
49.16	veranda	verandah
49.22	"Deerslayer"	Deerslayer
50.30	lake shore	Lake shore
51.9	lake shores	Lake shores
57.11	Shakspeare	Shakespeare
57.22	strangely.	strangely,
61.22	railroad	Railroad
61.23	lake shore	Lake shore
61.27	lake shore	Lake shore
61.31	railroad	Railroad

Village Improvement Societies

64.8	May-pole	Maypole
65.14	Shakspeare	Shakespeare
68.25	verandas	verandahs
74.9	branch	bunch

Otsego Leaves I: Birds Then and Now

81.26	wondered	wonder
81.28	11th	IIth
83.13	blue-bird	bluebird
83.28	chicadees	chickadees

Otsego Leaves II: The Bird Mediæval

89.30	half-wild	half wild
92.29	blue-bird	bluebird
93.13–14	blue-bird	bluebird
96.10	blue-birds	bluebirds

Otsego Leaves III: The Bird Primeval

102.21	blue-bird	bluebird
109.9	lake shore	lake-shore

Lament for the Birds

113.4	blue-birds	bluebirds
113.12	chicadees	chickadees

Textual Notes

Introduction to *Country Rambles*

21.24:   The phrase "where they" is centered in the original.

Introduction to *The Rhyme and Reason of Country Life*

Seven author's notes appear as footnotes in the original, included in the anthology; we have not reproduced those notes. We have assigned the remaining notes a sequence of superscripts and moved them to the end of the essay.

38.23:   As originally published, the phrase "the earth and all its holds" is difficult. It is possible that Cooper intended "holds" as a noun in the sense of "strongholds"; this, however, results in so anomalous a reading that we emend to "the earth and all it holds."

Village Improvement Societies

74.9:   The word "branch" occurs in two of the three different copies of *Putnam's Magazine* (September 1869) we consulted for this edition, but in one copy the word "bunch" occurs in place of "branch." The first definition of "bunch" as a noun in *The Dictionary of Americanisms* (ed. Mitford M. Mathews [Chicago: University of Chicago Press, 1951]) is a "clump of trees"; however, the word seems always to precede a prepositional phrase, e.g., "a bunch of maples." Since the word does not occur here with a defining prepositional phrase, and since this would be the only occurrence of "bunch" meaning a "clump of trees" in all of Cooper's published work, we take "bunch" as a typesetting error that was corrected to "branch" at some point in the printing of this issue of *Putnam's*.

Otsego Leaves II: The Bird Mediæval

88.16
and
94.4:

The two occurrences of "All-bonny" in this essay are the only two occurrences of this dialect pronunciation of "Albany" in all of Cooper's writings, and both times it is hyphenated at the end of a line. Without further evidence, it is not clear whether Cooper intended "All-bonny" or "Allbonny." We use the hyphenated form in case it is intended to stress an exaggerated pronunciation.

A Lament for the Birds

112.8:

The date "June 8, 1847" seems to be in error. Cooper first published an account of the flock of passenger pigeons confused by a fog in *Rural Hours*, as her entry for Friday, June 8. In her preface to that book, she reports that she began making her notes for *Rural Hours* "in the spring of 1848," which suggests that the year 1847 in this essay is wrong; the year would be either 1848 or 1849. If Friday is the correct day of the week, the year would be 1849, since June 8 fell on a Friday that year.

Explanatory Notes

A Dissolving View

4.30   "richest lake": a reddish pigment made from lac or cochineal, or by combining animal, vegetable, or coal-tar coloring with a metallic oxide.

6.19   "Righi-Kulm": a mountain peak above Switzerland's Lake Lucerne.

8.30   "valley of Tivoli": Tivoli is a city in central Italy, a favorite destination of eighteenth and nineteenth-century travelers because of its picturesque setting and classical and Renaissance architecture and landscape design.

8.32   "the Campagna": a lowland plain surrounding the city of Rome, abandoned until the mid–nineteenth century to marshes and malaria. With the Tyrrhenian Sea to its southwest, its other three sides are surrounded by mountains.

9.8   "Pæstum": a coastal city of southern Italy, famous for its well-preserved walls and Doric temples.

11.23   "the cave of Machpelah": the cave at Hebron purchased by Abraham as a family burial site (Genesis 23).

12.20   "grand Palace of Glass, now standing in London": the large exhibition hall built largely of glass and iron, otherwise referred to as the "Crystal Palace." It opened on May 1, 1851, and was later moved to Sydenham Hill in southeastern London, where it was completed in 1854.

12.25   "Daguerre": Louis Jacques Mandé Daguerre (1789–1851), painter and codeveloper of the daguerreotype, an early photographic method that used metal plates.

13.4   "Monsieur Agassiz": Louis Agassiz (1807–73), Swiss-born
             naturalist, at Harvard from 1848. One of his century's most
             influential promoters of the natural sciences, he opposed Dar-
             win's theory of natural selection, believing that Christian tele-
             ology explained speciation.

14.1   "architectural consequences": *Consequences* is a parlor game
             played in a round. One player starts a narrative of the meeting
             of a lady and a gentleman, and others in turn continue the narra-
             tive, adding the ensuing "consequences" of this initial meeting.

14.2   "wych-hazel": witch hazel, the popular name of several decid-
             uous shrubs of the genus *Hamamelis*; a forked branch of witch
             hazel was commonly used as a divining rod for locating under-
             ground water.

Introduction to *Country Rambles*

18.10   " 'The smooth Severn stream' ": Milton, *Comus*, line 825.

18.12–13   " 'Rush-yfringed bank . . .' ": sung by Sabrina, the goddess of
             the river Severn. Milton, *Comus*, lines 890–91.

18.15   "at the foot of Plinlimnon": The Plynlimon Mountains are in
             central Wales.

19.17–26   " 'Still she retains . . .' ": Milton, *Comus*, lines 842–51.

21.17–18   " 'Certain . . . Normand' ": literally, "a certain Gascon fox,
             that others call Norman."

21.21–23   " 'The temple-loving martlet . . .' ": Shakespeare, *Macbeth*,
             I.vi.4–6. Shakespeare's martlet is rather "temple-haunting,"
             and its nest building is referred to as "mansionry," not "man-
             sioning."

21.25–26   " 'Most breed, and haunt . . .' ": Shakespeare, *Macbeth*, I.vi.9–
             10.

21.28–29   " 'Sings darkling . . .' ": Milton, *Paradise Lost*, book III, lines 39–40.

22.1   " 'The herald of the morn' ": Shakespeare, *Romeo and Juliet*, III.v.6.

23.7   "S. F. Baird": Spencer Fullerton Baird (1823–87), much-published American naturalist.

23.8   "Major Le Conte": John Eatton Le Conte (1784–1860), American naturalist; among various studies, published works on native grape vines, pecans, and tobacco; an accomplished entomologist as well.

23.8   "M. A. Curtis": Moses Ashley Curtis (1808–1872), American botanist.

Introduction to *The Rhyme and Reason of Country Life*

26.10   "vale of Tempe": a five-mile-long river gorge in northern Thessaly.

26.10   "Hymettus": one of the four mountain systems dominating the Attican landscape.

28.16   "the familiar name": Cooper alludes to the extraordinarily popular "The Seasons" by the British poet James Thomson.

28.18   "cotemporary": With the exception of one occurrence in "A Dissolving View" (9), only in this essay does Cooper use this rare word. It is not included in the *Oxford English Dictionary*. It is regularly used, however, in Elise C. Otté's translation of Alexander von Humboldt's *Cosmos: A Sketch of a Physical Description of the Universe*.

32.9   "The Canticle of the Three Children": Also entitled "The Song of the Three Young Men," this book of the Apocrypha contains the liturgical song of the three Jewish captives in Babylon thrown into the fiery furnace for refusing to worship Nebuchadnezzar's golden image (Daniel 3).

34.26 "merle and mavis": poetic terms for a blackbird and a thrush noted usually for their beautiful songs. The phrase "merle and mavis" generally echoes the popular poetry of Scott and Burns. In her annotations to *Country Rambles*, Cooper identifies "merle" as "turdus merula" and "mavis" as "turdus musicus" (302–3).

34.31 "Arcite": one of the two prisoners in love with Emilia in Chaucer's "The Knight's Tale" and in Dryden's "Palamon and Arcite."

36.7 "Madame du Deffand": Mme du Deffand, Marie de Vichy-Chamrond (1697–1780), French literary hostess and longtime friend to Horace Walpole. Many of her letters to Walpole were published.

36.8–9 " 'Je . . . innocents!' ": literally, "I don't care for innocent pleasures."

38.31 " 'For thy pleasure . . .' ": Revelation 4:11.

39.20 "a greater than Homer": specifically the psalmist. Cooper pieces her quotation together by borrowing from Psalms 29:2 and 33:8.

39.22 "Mr. Keble": John Keble (1792–1866), British poet and clergyman, professor of poetry at Oxford, 1831–41.

44.2 " 'Non . . . monaco!' ": literally, "It is not from the habit that a monk is made"; or, "Clothes don't make the man."

Preface to the 1868 *Rural Hours*

46.6–7 " 'nous . . . cela' ": literally, "we have changed all of that."
46.14 "afrite": afreet, a monstrous demon of Arabic myths.

Later Hours

47.15 "Gessler": In Switzerland's legend of William Tell, Gessler is the cruel Austrian bailiff who arrested Tell and then forced the

Swiss hero to shoot an arrow at an apple placed on his young son's head. Tell's second arrow killed Gessler.

47.17   "Niobe": In Greek mythology, Niobe has many children, usually either twelve or fourteen. When she claims to be equal to the Titaness Leto by virtue of her many births, Leto's two children, Apollo and Artemis, kill Niobe's children. Niobe's grief over her children is a stock type of bereavement in Western art.

49.28   "a little cottage was built": Byberry Cottage was built for Cooper and her sister Anne Charlotte after the deaths of their parents in 1851 and 1852. Some materials from the recently burned Otsego Hall were used in building the cottage. Otsego Hall, completed in 1799, was built by Cooper's grandfather, Judge William Cooper. James Fenimore Cooper lost the Hall to debts in 1822 but repurchased it in 1834. Shortly after the family sold it in 1852, it burned. Cooper lived in Byberry Cottage until her death.

53.29   "W. Mudie": an error for Robert Mudie (1777–1842), author of *The Feathered Tribes of the British Islands* (London: Whittaker and Company, 1835), from which Cooper quotes this passage on the skylark. Inaccuracies in the quotation, however, show that she relied upon her original use of this passage in her appendix to *Country Rambles*, not on Mudie's text.

55.1   "Charles Fox": Charles James Fox (1749–1806), British statesman and author of many volumes of speeches and nonfiction.

58.6   "Paley": William Paley (1743–1805), British natural theologian, author of *Natural Theology* (1802) and other works.

Village Improvement Societies

65.15   "Hobbinol and Lobbinol": Hobbinol and Lobin are shepherd names in Spenser's *The Shepheards Calender*; Cooper alters the latter for comic rhyme with Hobbinol.

65.15   "Diggory": a common name for a farcical character, occurring, for example, in Goldsmith's *She Stoops to Conquer* (1773).

65.15   "Mopsa and Dorcas": shepherdesses in Shakespeare's *The Winter's Tale*.

65.16   "scarcely knowing B from bullsfoot": a common and old expression indicating that a person knows very little.

65.20   "our Huguenot ancestors": Cooper's great-great-grandfather Étienne De Lancey was a Huguenot. He fled to England in 1685 after Louis XIV revoked the Edict of Nantes.

66.7   "Madame de Sévigné": Marie de Rabutin-Chantal Sévigné (1626–96), French writer best known for her letters, which vividly chronicle her life among the highest social and court circles in seventeenth-century France.

66.12   " 'C'est le bon Dieu' ": In this context, "It is the work of God!"

67.20–21   "the wines of Delmonico": Delmonico's was a very fashionable restaurant on Fifth Avenue in New York City.

67.21   "the diamonds of Ball & Black": Ball & Black's was a New York City jewelry store and rival of Tiffany's.

70.13   "salamander safes": a fireproof iron safe, whose manufacture began in 1833.

73.14   "playstow": a place of play, a playground. *The Oxford English Dictionary* gives this word as "local" and not common in modern English. The only two modern occurrences of "playstow" given are from Gilbert White's *Antiquities* (1789) and Mortimer Collins' *Thoughts in My Garden* (1876), where the author discusses a memorial to Gilbert White.

Otsego Leaves I: Birds Then and Now

83.13   "greenlet": a vireo.

83.13	"yellow-bird": the yellow warbler.
84.28	"Croton": a water supply that superseded the town pump; so called from New York City's use of the Croton River in Westchester County for its water supply beginning in 1842.
86.19	"rice-birds": This term has been applied to several species of small birds that visited the Southern rice fields, but especially the bobolink.

Otsego Leaves II: The Bird Mediæval

88.2	"the Flats": now the New York town of Watervliet, on the Hudson River near Troy.
88.19	"caudle-feasts": A caudle was a warm spiced drink containing wine or ale prepared mainly for the sick or for women in childbed and their visitors.
91.19	"colonel and madam": In her biographical sketch of Mrs. Philip Schuyler, Cooper indirectly identifies this couple as "Colonel Philip Schuyler of the 'Flats,' and his admirable wife—'Madam' to the world at large. . . ." This Philip Schuyler was a "near relative" of the Revolutionary War figure she writes about in the sketch. The colonel of "Otsego Leaves" died in 1757; "Madam" continued to live at the Flats. ("Mrs. Philip Schuyler: A Sketch." In *Worthy Women of Our First Century*. Ed. Mrs. O. J. Wister and Miss Agnes Irwin. Philadelphia: J. B. Lippincott and Co., 1877. 71–111.)
	Since Cooper published the sketch in the year before "The Bird Mediæval," the opening sentence of the later essay suggests that it was while researching the Schuyler biography ("in looking over old records or family legends of colonial years") that she "gather[ed] glimpses of bird-life" from her sources to create at least this one of the four "Otsego Leaves" essays.

Otsego Leaves III: The Bird Primeval

99.21   "stag-horns": staghorn sumac, so called for its antler-like
         branches.

100.6   "amelanchier": the genus of shrubs and small trees that includes
         all the species and varieties of the Juneberry, which Cooper fre-
         quently mentions in *Rural Hours*.

A Lament for the Birds

113.7   "gold-crests": gold-crowned kinglets.

113.7   "ruby-crowns": ruby-crowned kinglets.

113.13   "gray snow-birds": slate-colored juncos.

Index

Dante Alighieri, 35
Deffand, Madame du, 36
"Dissolving View, A," xiv–xv, 3–16
Dresden, 74
Dryden, John, 55, 56

education, American, 60–61

Felix, Minucius, 32
"Flats, the," 87–96 passim
Fox, Charles James, 55
Fox of Lafontaine, 21

Goethe, Johann Wolfgang von, 30
Greek art, nature in ancient, 25–27
Gregory, St., 31

Herbert, George, 52, 64
history, wilderness, 97–109 passim
Home Book of the Picturesque, The,
    xv
honey bee, 57–58
house-wren, 78, 79–80
Humboldt, Alexander von,
    xvii–xviii; quoted, 25, 27, 28
humming-bird, 78–79

ignorance, in America of plant and
    animal species, 20–22

Kalidasa, 28
Keble, John, xix, 39
Knapp, John Leonard, xiv, xv, xxix,
    17, 19–20, 22–23, 48

"Lament for the Birds, A,"
    xxvii–xxviii, 110–14
landscape, American, 3–5, 13;
    differences from Old World, 11,
    14–16, 19; human abuses of, 6;
    human presence preferred on,
    5–6
lark, voice of, 53–54
"Later Hours," xix–xxi, 47–63
laurel, 51
Le Conte, John Eatton, 23
Lieu-schew, 29
Lind, Jenny, 80
"Little Red Riding Hood," 21
Louis XI, 9

Machpelah, cave of, 11
Milton, John: quoted, 18, 19, 21
mounds, European, 7
Mudie, Robert: quoted, 53–54

nature: appreciation of, in
    American poetry, 41; in Chinese
    literature, 28–29; in Christian
    literature, 31–39; in Greek and
    Roman literature, 24–28; in
    Hebrew literature, 29–31; in
    Sanscrit literature, 28; in work of
    troubadours, 34–35
nature writing: education and
    Christian revelation necessary
    for, 37–39; value of, 17, 20
"negroes, Dutch," 87–96 passim
nightingale, 54–57
North American continent, 13

Odyssey, 55, 56
Otsego Hall, 49
"Otsego Leaves," xxii–xxvii,
    78–109

Palace of Glass, 12
Paley, William, 58
pelican, white, 110–11
Penn, William, 71
Petrarch, 35
pigeon, passenger, 53, 111–12
pine, white, 110
Putnam, George, xv

railroad, 45–46, 52, 61–62
Reingold, Nathan, xxix
Rhyme and Reason of Country Life,
    Introduction to, xiv, xvi–xix,
    24–44
Righi-Kulm, 6
robin: nest attacked by hawk, 47–49;
    nesting of, 49–50, 51–52, 59,
    80–81
Rural Hours, xiii, xiv, xv, xvii,
    xx, xxi, xxiii–xxiv, xxv, xxviii;
    Preface to 1868 edition, 45–46
rural life: more civilizing than
    urban, 36–37, 40–44; poetry of,
    as a superior form, 39–40

Schiller, Friedrich von: quoted,
    24–25

"Seasons, The," 36
See-ma-kuang, 28–29
Severn River, 18
Sévigné, Marie de Rabutin-Chantal,
    marquise de, 66
spring, 4
street names, 71–72
sublime, in landscape, 6–7
summer, 5
Susquehanna River, 45, 52
swallow, barn, 90–91, 113–14
swan, 111
swift, chimney, 113; nesting in
    ancient elm, 98–109 passim;
    twig-gathering method of, 103–4

"Te Deum," 32

"Village Improvement Societies,"
    xxi–xxii, 64–77
village improvement society, work
    of, 68–77
village life: differences between
    European and American, 64–68;
    importance of, xxii

water lilies, 50
White, Gilbert, xiii, 17–18
Wilson, Alexander, 111
winter, 5
Wordsworth, William, 35–36
Wright, Mabel Osgood, xxix